# Heartful Journeys: Exploring The Power Of Mindful Living

Book Wave Publications

Published by Book Wave Publications, 2023.

While every precaution has been taken in the preparation of this book, the publisher assumes no responsibility for errors or omissions, or for damages resulting from the use of the information contained herein.

HEARTFUL JOURNEYS: EXPLORING THE POWER OF MINDFUL LIVING

**First edition. September 6, 2023.**

Copyright © 2023 Book Wave Publications.

ISBN: 979-8223850397

Written by Book Wave Publications.

# Also by Book Wave Publications

How To Make Money In Stocks Value Investing Strategies
Master The Steps To Move Away From The Past And
Following Inspiration
Heartful Journeys: Exploring The Power Of Mindful Living

# Table of Contents


What You'll Discover ............................................................. 1

About The Book.................................................................... 2

Who This Book Is For............................................................ 4

Introduction......................................................................... 5

Personal Strength Test ......................................................... 9

Talents and Skills................................................................ 12

How Does The Brain Produce Talents?................................ 18

Nature's Destructive Cycle.................................................. 22

How Does The Brain Generate Abilities? ............................ 28

The Destructive Cycle Of Nature........................................ 32

Parents Ought To Comprehend........................................... 38

Recognizing Talent.............................................................. 41

Pregnancy's Seventh Month And The Appearance Of Talent.................................................................................. 46

One Of A Kind Prenatal Spiritual Intervention .................. 55

Mind And Matter ............................................................... 62

A Personality For Altitude................................................... 68

Biology Is Influenced By Belief............................................ 79

Criminals Do Not Appear Out Of Nowhere .......................... 86

Most Ideal Environment For An Existence .......................... 88

Analysis Of A Case ............................................ 91

A Man Is Made By His Mind .................................. 96

Education And Inspiration ...................................... 100

Education Weakens Inherent Intelligence ........................ 104

Journaling For Self-Reflection .................................. 107

# Heartful Journeys: Exploring The Power Of Mindful Living

## Overcoming Stress, Building Personal Power & Finding Joy Steps To A Happier And More Mindful Way Of Living

# What You'll Discover

1. Knowing how stress and anxiety function
2. acquiring coping mechanisms to deal with stress
3. figuring out how to live each day with more joy and happiness
4. Building self-confidence through practising mindfulness
5. Changing negative thought patterns to promote a more positive outlook

# About The Book

Personal Development, Personal Transformation, and Finding Your Life Purpose - All humans grapple with these topics, but only some create a meaningful process for living life to its full potential. This is the longest, most thorough, and detailed Personal Development and Personal Transformation Book available on this platform!

We live in a modern world of overabundance everywhere. We face an overabundance of stimulation and content coming at us from our cell phones and screens. We are drowning in an overabundance of stuff, junk, and possessions that arrive cheaply and near-instantly from Amazon and your favourite superstore. And we are overwhelmed with giant portions of fat and sugar-filled food and snacks made available to us every waking moment.

Modern overabundance is fueled by a digital delivery system that makes traditional self-help techniques impotent. In the modern, attention-driven economy, everybody is fighting for our mind space. This Book will teach you how to aggressively take back control of your own mind, your own habits, and your own creativity by counter-programming your brain with your own wipes, dreams and goals.

The world is splitting into two groups at greater acceleration: The creators versus the consumers, those who take action versus those who are passive, the haves versus the have-nots, the fulfilled versus the empty, the ones who create a lasting legacy and those who are soon forgotten.

Which group do you want to be a part of?

You can take 100% control over your present and future. You have the ability to condition your thoughts, actions, and methods of living life for more fulfilling results.

If you are ready to live a more active life, develop your own creative projects and live a healthier and more meaningful life, then Read today for this Complete Personal Development Personal Transformation Guide.

# Who This Book Is For

1. Ambitious leaders
2. Individuals who want more out of life
3. Learners who want a more fulfilling life
4. Anyone stuck in a rut looking to get to a higher level
5. Individuals looking for tools for Managing Burnout
6. C-level executives
7. Anyone looking for Best Practices for Reducing Stress

# Introduction

There is a particular type of bamboo tree in China that, when buried in soil, only sprouts one stem above the surface. Farmers carefully tend to it by watering, fertilising, pulling weeds, and performing other farming tasks. But what really occurs? Even after a full year has passed, the bamboo shoot looks unharmed by all the love and attention it has gotten.

Does the Chinese farmer give up because he is dissatisfied with the outcome of his labours? No. He continues to fervently nourish the sprout by adding more water, manure, fertilisers, etc. In addition, he observes that the bamboo shoot appears to be still sleeping and indifferent, not sharing his escalating zeal or curiosity.

The shoot also doesn't move forward at all at the conclusion of the second year! The farmer should take it out and replace it, a sceptic recommended. He views the farmer as an example of fortitude, despite the fact that the farmer's 'non-stimulated' bamboo shoot at the end of the third and fourth years doesn't deter him either. The Bhagavad Gita extols the virtue of "Karmanye vadhikaraste, ma phaleshu kadachana" (Your job is merely to carry out the assigned work, not worrying about its fruits).

But pause. In the fifth year, the shoot abruptly shakes itself up and begins to spread as if it had just woken up after a lengthy nap. And lo! You have an 80-foot-tall bamboo tree by the end of the fifth year, majestically surveying the horizon and announcing to the world, "I have arrived."

Why does the bamboo shoot not respond to food after four years of getting all the growth-promoting inputs? and then soared the following year? In this situation, nature is teaching us a crucial lesson. How is it possible for a tree to stand straight above the ground and endure any unfavourable climatic conditions, such as a flood, drought, hailstorm, etc., if it isn't supported by a very strong root system that is deeply and firmly rooted in the soil?

When the active "groundwork" was complete, the young shoot above ground spent the first four years of its existence working to establish a network of strong and powerful roots so that it might grow outdoors and stand tall and erect as a mighty and enduring tree. Call it the agricultural law.

How much there is to learn from nature doesn't need to be emphasised. achievement on the outside should follow inside achievement. Your own development and improvement should come first. a good illustration of a person who has matured within. Any superstructure would be weak and prone to falling at the first sign of trouble without a sturdy base. One must first work on themselves before venturing out into the world to attain success in the public eye. The key to success is this.

The gross body and the subtle body are the two different types of bodies we have. The former, which is the outer one, is composed of five parts. The interior body of the latter is composed of the mind, intellect, and ego. The subtle body is home to the soul or spirit. Unfortunately, a lot of people still feed their ego because they mistakenly believe it to be a true reflection of who they are. When this occurs, the ego obstructs and conceals the mind, weakening it and hiding the true inner self.

Recall that the limitless spirit that is within you and me joined us in the seventh month of our mother's womb and will be with us always. It acts as our only companion for the rest of our life, in a way. Apart from the ego, which is fundamentally flawed, only the two faculties of the subtle body—an awakened mind and a discriminating intellect—can be employed to cultivate the inner self and attain self-development.

Do you remember how the Kadopanishad compares the intellect to the charioteer and the mind to the reins in its hands via which the horses, or sensory organs, are adequately controlled and directed? Your inner potential is awakened and a fulfilling existence is achieved when you live intentionally. In order to connect with the inner life energy known as the self, the intellect will guide and empower the mind.

The first book in a series on holistic human development has the working title "Boundless Power of Mindful Living." Reading the book is entertaining and simple because it is written in the manner of classroom talks between a trainer and his students. As readers read the content, this type of organisation also aims to clarify any questions and doubts they may have.

The critical significance of spiritual development, which is essential for a person's overall growth and evolution, is also covered. Some of the high points include the stage of the spirit's entry into the foetal body, the deterministic changes in the brain that begin in the seventh month of pregnancy, an exceptional spiritual intervention used in an Ashram to support the talents at the foetal stage, the significance of the mindset, and everyday habits that need to be unlearned for successful parenting. When the text of the book was evaluated by the online writing tool "Grammarly," it was found to be "very clear" and "very engaging."

# Personal Strength Test

It was a Book on enhancing soft skills for individual growth. The trainer, Anandavardhan, was disclosing the secret to success in all spheres of life. Knowledge, skill, and talent are the constituent parts of a person's strength. On the whiteboard, he drew three circles: two that were parallel and overlapped, and one that was in the middle and below the other two.

Your strength lies at the intersection of the three, Anandavardhen said. Knowledge is never generated; it is always discovered. It goes as follows: The first is the knowledge you gain from Books like this one, reputable books, seminars, and other resources. Student of medicine named Supriya. She pursues studies in the sciences, including pharmacology, gynaecology, anatomy, physiology.

Excuse me, sir, while I ask a question. Will a person's overall strength suffer if two of the three elements of strength are extraordinarily strong but the third is only marginally so?Lal, that is a nice question. For the strength to increase, all three are necessary. If aptitude and skill are good but information is lacking, the performance will be, at best, subpar. Consider a skilled and experienced painter who is new to the medium.

His knowledge or abilities will be of little use if he doesn't know that combining green and red paint will produce a brown tint. A specialist in lighting design, on the other hand, should be aware that the combination of red and green light produces the colour yellow rather than brown. When that happens, having sufficient knowledge is essential. Of sufficient intellect and ability, too.What is the second type of knowledge, sir? useful information or expertise. This knowledge is superior to that learned from books and other sources. It is perpetual.

We live life forward and understand it backward, according to a philosopher. That knowledge is based on personal observation. Experience, according to Aldous Huxley, is not what happens to you. What matters is what you do with the things that happen to you. Anthony Gell's "Book of Leadership" may be summed up in one question: "What is the secret of your success?" The interviewer questioned a successful bank president. Two words, he uttered.

What are the two words, then?

"Wise choices"

How do you make informed choices?

"One word," the President said.

What is that one word exactly?

"Experience," "Sir, how do you acquire experience?"

What does the phrase "two words" mean in this situation?

"Wrong choices"Everyone in the class started laughing.

According to a book, Kahlil Gibran once stated, "I learned silence from the talkative, tolerance from the intolerant, and kindness from the unkind." Sandeep added a bit. But I do respect these teachers. We take lessons from our failures and mistakes. They are our teachers; we must respect and believe in them. They deserve our respect and admiration. The talented people among us do just that; they follow these 'teachers'' instructions and climb the success ladder.

Malathi Varma, a follower of the Guru, said, "Sir, but a spiritual master, and his words can be understood only from out of the experience." Knowing from experience is special since it cannot be expressed in words or written about in books. Malathi said as much. Why haven't we heard it straight from the source, if that's the case? In order to demonstrate Malathi's devotion to his spiritual Master, Anandavardhan added: "I'll get to that in the Book of our conversation.

The lecturer brought up the subject once more, saying, "Strictly speaking, knowledge itself is founded on experience. As I just mentioned, whether through instruction or observation, it must always be learned. While schooling, training, reading, listening, and other ways can be used to acquire knowledge and facts, experiential knowledge must be actively pursued and observed. Our mistakes and failures serve as our teachers in the later group.

# Talents and Skills

The second pillar of strength, which is concerned with skills, is next. Skill is the capacity to carry out specific tasks quickly, almost faultlessly, and with ease. The practice method is another way to learn it. To dance, draw, write stories and poetry, act on stage, and more, you need specific skills. There are, Of course, more factors.As a result, skill is the response to the query "how?" Certainly not, Sir? Lal made a note.

"Right. Which inquiries, Lal, will result in the answer "knowledge"?

"What, Why, When, and Where," he uttered.

"Correct".

"Talent is the third component for increasing strength. What do you think talent is?

According to Sandeep, it is the ability to carry out particular activities very well.That refers to the quality of the work that talent produces. What is meant by talent is explained by the approach. How does it become obvious? A "pattern of thought, feeling, or behaviour that recurs naturally and can be used profitably" is what is meant by the term talent.

Could you define "naturally recurring"? Cannot be accomplished through one's own initiative or willpower?" Thomsen enquired. "Exactly. The distinction between talent, skill, and knowledge is made at that point. We are aware that education and training can come from several sources. but not the talents, which must be cultivated through study and practice and must come from inside. The instructor responded.

Do you mean "innate nature," sir? There is a tiny difference. The cumulative "samskara," or inherent character, also known as "vasana," is the outcome of the karmas of prior incarnations. Do you recall in Malathi what our Guru said in the holy text regarding this?

Certainly, sir. According to the Guruvani, one's jiva (spirit or soul) manifests "vasana" as a result of their natural virtues and vices (punya and papa).The punya and papa of a person display the characteristics of their jiva.

Sandeep was commanded, "Sir, explain the meaning of the word samskara." "Everything that accumulates from previous lifetimes in the human psyche will become a predisposition. It speaks of a propensity or propensity to act or move in a certain way. Habits, which are the audible expressions of your samskara, will be formed as a result of the combination of these mental impressions.

In other words, it is necessary to think of innate nature as an intuitive consciousness that is untaught rather than instructive. In contrast to scholarship, which must be learned, vasana is what comes naturally. Contrary to innate nature, or vasana, which is a propensity, knowledge and skill are instructive.OK. Thus, vasana is the product of earlier karmas. How does talent develop?

The connections in the brain lead to recurring patterns of thinking, emotion, or behaviour. That implies the inheritance of talent and inherent talent across families, doesn't it? They do naturally occur. Both are inventions of the mind. But there is no longer any resemblance. These two are étiologically separate. We learned that the jiva's vasana is an accumulation of previous karmic effects. Genius arises from the connections made by brain cells, even if it is congenital. Both use their innate talents to further their aptitudes and attitudes, which makes them comparable.

Do you believe that aptitude and aptitude go hand in hand, sir? Supriya expressed interest. Talent is the capacity to complete specified activities swiftly and competently, as we just discussed. It becomes increasingly sophisticated as a result of the practical experience gained through consistent practice. Skills provide a framework and real-world understanding.

However, excellence can only be achieved when it is backed from behind by talent, regardless of the level or standard of the skill. In other words, "talents decide how well and how often a person can do a certain thing, while skills decide whether a person can do a certain thing."

For instance, a female without talent cannot become an accomplished dancer, artist, or vocalist even with persistence and hard work. If you lack the skill for writing, even with correct grammar, it could be challenging for you to do it well.

Although skill is necessary for success, competence by itself won't make you a household name. You stated, sir, that skills cannot be improved alone by study or practice. Please provide more details. Remya enquired.

"Sure. As I've already stated, the formation of skills is a result of brain connections. We are unable to comprehend, want, or manage the actions that the brain takes. The connections between neurons are fixed and cannot be altered. Once more, the inherent attributes and skills (vasana) are comparable. Both should be applied in their exact form throughout one's life.

In other words, regulating your strength necessitates focusing only on information and talent. Supriya took note of it. That doesn't mean you have no responsibilities or power in your field of expertise. Anandavardhan claims that realising your potential entails recognizing naturally occurring patterns of thinking, emotion, or behaviour and supplying them with the necessary information and abilities.

According to Supriya, this strengthens the connections between brain cells.

There are further strategies for bolstering one's skills and assets. The question is, "What are they, Sir?"One of the foremost experts on employee productivity in the world, Marcus Buckingham, suggests that you start by identifying and carefully considering your values. If you discover that your interests and values are elsewhere, embrace them by altering your lifestyle.

What issue is most important to you? Which is preferable, joining a charity to give back or starting a business to make money? Since your values reside in the latter, if you strive for it, you'll discover your purpose and passion. You are probably employing a talent if you like doing something.

Self-awareness is a way to connect with your talents. Your ability to recognize your talents grows as you become more self-aware. It is simpler to cultivate your strengths after you have identified them. Self-awareness will be covered in more detail in a later session.

In general, skills are innate human abilities that cannot be learnt. A talent cannot be created; it can only be improved or diminished. But I must mention that this matter is being addressed spiritually in the Ashram that Malathi and I frequently attend.

They all turned to face Malathi as she approached. At her expression of bewilderment and confusion, Anandavardhan laughed. He enquired, "Malathi, has your sister returned from the States?"Sure, sir. It has been instructed for her to appear at the Ashram for the "Sankalpa."Sankalpa? Describe that. Supriya enquired with worry.

Anandavardhan explained, "That is a particular spiritual practice done when women are carrying, in the seventh month of pregnancy.I'm sorry, sir, but we've gotten off topic. Sandeep snuck in, "We're interested in knowing what the Ashram is doing in the area of talent development. It's not like we're shifting the subject, Sandeep. Actually, we are entering that area.

By discussing Sankalpa, a pregnant woman's prayers, or anything else.ExactlyEverything seems to be switching over to Latin and Greek. Right now, nothing is being recorded.Sandeep, just be patient. cling on. To better understand what occurs in our brains, the place where the seeds of our talents are sown, let's first take a closer look at them.

# How Does The Brain Produce Talents?

The trainer claimed that before beginning to contract with ageing, our brains first expand more swiftly than other organs. It is really fascinating to consider how IQ and brain size relate to one another.

The class was attentive as the scientific exposition began. After 42 days, the first brain nerve cell forms in the embryo. It is known as a "neuron." Then, an exponential growth results in the production of 9500 new neurons every second. 120 days after the first neuron is generated, there are 100 billion neurons in the world.Wow! Who can answer the question, "What is the value of a billion?" The teacher changed the focus of the inquiry to include everyone in the group.

One million is ten lakh, therefore what is a billion? According to Anandavardhan, "a billion is a million times a million." In the US, it is one hundred crore. In English, it means one lakh crore.

At 162 days, the foetus has 100 billion neurons, and this number does not rise. No matter how old the person grows, their birth number remains the same.

The fact that there aren't many neurons is unimportant. Just sixty days before birth, the baby's brain starts to go through some astounding changes. The 100 billion nerve cells are now starting to join after being scattered and disconnected previously.

"How does it happen?" is the pertinent query. Synapses, also known as docking sites, are what connect neurons together while axons, which resemble long, finger-like nerve fibres, connect neurons to one another. I think you need to go into this a little bit more, sir.

I will then elaborate. All operations of the nervous system begin with neurons. Despite the fact that there are many different types of neurons, axons and dendrites are the two fundamental types of extensions that all neurons have. Neurons may communicate with one another thanks to their axons, which are long, finger-like nerve fibres, and dendrites, which are brief branching projects from the cell body.

The real locations of interaction between neurons are 'docking points' (synapses) on the surface of the dendrites, where axons from other cells link with them. Despite the fact that many of them have numerous dendrites and docking sites, the bulk of nerve cells only have one axon. Axons send impulses, which are received by dendrites.

You ask, "What are these signals?" "An electrical charge wave that moves from the cell body to the axon is referred to as a signal. Each neuron serves as a miniature computer, comparing and evaluating data from different neurons to decide whether and how forcefully to "fire" and relay the signal.

Notably, neurons frequently prefer messages from other neurons who have a "track record" of providing "reliable" information. A single neuron can receive input from up to one lakh neurons. It will choose which signals to pay attention to and which to ignore after reviewing the data. It is incredible how a signal may pass through a vast network of cells, activate the brain, and then represent a thought, a sensation, or a perception together with the resulting behaviour.

"Marvellous. And we are blissfully unaware of all these clever decisions that our brain cells are making every second, Remya continued. Remya was stunned and unable to speak.

The teacher remarked, "Really, that's how the Creator planned and designed the super computer called the brain." It is critical to remember that our brain constantly adds and deletes connections between neurons, alters the strength of existing ones, and creates new neural connections. A synapse's capacity, personality, or docking point might change as a result of experience.

We lack the knowledge necessary to completely understand how the brain works. Knowing that our behaviour is influenced by the proper connections between neurons is sufficient. In other words, the patterns of recurrent thought, sensation, or behaviour that make up your synapses, which are essentially what cause your abilities, are what cause them.

Axons, which start developing sixty days before the baby is born, link neurons together. Up until the infant is three years old, this process continues throughout the early years of life. By the end of the third year, each of the 100 billion neurons will have formed 15,000 synaptic connections with other nerve cells. By doing this, you will establish a pattern and map for your skills over the Book of your life. The entire class was busy taking notes and paying attention to the understudied topic of talent development.

# Nature's Destructive Cycle

"Okay, pay close attention as I continue to speak. The brain then goes through an unexpected occurrence. That will manifest as an odd 12-year process of annihilation. Nature won't notice the vast majority of the densely braided neural filaments. As a child and adolescent, you will inevitably form the habit of disregarding many synaptic connections in your brain.

How will these unused connections be handled? They will wear out, break, and degrade with time. A chunk of the child's brain network will start to be broken up, deleted, and obliterated after the age of three. Between the ages of four and fifteen, a child will lose billions upon billions of the intricately woven brain connections. By the time the teen awakens to celebrate his sixteenth birthday, half of the brain network, which started to emerge in the seventh month of pregnancy and proceeded through the fourth year of life, will have been irrevocably damaged.

Do you mean hurt beyond repair, sir? There is no doubt about that. Afterward, no additional synapses will develop? After the age of 15, the brain will still retain some of its youthful plasticity, Of course. For instance, anytime you learn something new or develop a new skill, a new synaptic connection will appear in your brain.

Your approach to specific types of partial impairment, such as losing a leg, will affect how you weave new connections. But after the age of 15, the brain network's structure generally stays the same.Looks silly, sir. Why does nature behave so strangely? Why should it allow the well planned networking to last for more than three years before casually discarding half of it? Sandeep enquired.

"Let me share a wonderful bit of natural history with you. Early Sankhya philosophers referred to nature as "Prakriti" and "Avyakta," which is a more accurate term. Undifferentiated and non-manifested both fall under this category. True avyakta can be found in the human brain, one of nature's mysterious works of art. According to the Shvetashevatara Upanishad, Prakriti is once more utilised to create the concept of "Maya". Additionally, the "maya" of prakriti is manifested by the brain. In a scientific sense, nature is God, according to Swami Vivekananda. The word "nescience" is used to refer to ignorance or a lack of knowledge. Every name and form we use is a fabrication that reflects our ignorance.

In line with Vivekananda's philosophy of "less is more," this response, which will once again serve as a display of our ignorance, will not please us simple people who seek logic and reason in everything. Please be aware that there are limits to how much information our brain can handle at once. I'll soon provide you with a more robust and solid justification for the extensive brain network fading. Please wait.

It is important to realise that modern parents who lust after the newest technology in the belief that their kids will become wiser and more brilliant as a result of using them are living in a fool's paradise. By adding more synaptic connections to one's brain, one cannot become smarter or more intelligent. Creativity, productivity, and similar traits depend on how successfully brain connections are generated and utilised rather than only on numerical data.

However, Sir, how can you improve and maximise something that you are unable to recognize or identify? The Prakriti must be happy right now to hear your question, Sandeep. Nature is averting these issues by removing 50% of the synaptic connections that each of the 100 billion neurons make at a rate of 15,000 connections every second. so that we can concentrate on a smaller group of people in order to support and benefit the greatest people. Think of this as one of the reasons for Mother Nature's odd conduct in destroying a large number of connections.

Please remember that there is plenty for a youngster to learn about the outside world and that nature was nice enough to establish so many connections in the first place. However, only the child truly carries it out. Don't attempt to make sense of it; just soak it all in.

Why can the youngster only absorb things? Why can't it make sense of what it sees? The child's brain has a large number of synaptic connections, resulting in the child's brain having a large number of synaptic connections, which causes the child to be confused and overwhelmed by the flood of impulses from all directions. Unless and until a significant number of these signals are denied entry into the mind, the child will be inattentive in the middle of the overflowing messages in its brain. Over the following twelve years, nature will help break up a lot of unneeded connections. This might be connected to the second likely explanation for Prakriti's unusual "behaviour".

I concur, but how does it aid in the formation of the vital cerebral connections, sir?

Is it not a skill when a young child shows early aptitude for singing, dancing, painting, drawing, etc.? What is the source of it? from synapses that are most powerful. Similar to this, children's innate cognitive, mood, or behaviour patterns—like their focus on detail, foresight, capacity for planning, etc.—are an indication of the strength of their synaptic connections. When encouraged and frequently exposed to settings that are supportive, these attitudes and behaviours will increase the underlying network connections when they are reinforced both internally and externally.

The situation may be similar to this: The 'birth presents' the creator has given you resemble wrapped presents, much like the customary gifts we give or receive. Once you open the birth present packets God provided you and start using them in your daily life, God will keep bringing you more and more of these delightful gifts. As you encourage your child to show talent for singing or drawing, the girl gradually gets better at the performance, becomes an expert at it, and is given the term "gifted." This is a sign that the pleased God has been awarding her with "bonus gifts."

"Sir, what will happen to the idle connections on the network?" These will eventually pass away. What will happen to a knife if it sits untouched in a kitchen corner for a few months? Will it not corrode and lose its usefulness?

But is it not feasible that some of the weak network connections might eventually develop stronger in tandem with the preponderant ones, giving rise to the creation of a genius, provided nature is not permitted to intervene with the network and the brain is allowed to function on its own?

Though it's good to use your imagination, the results would be horrible, my love. Due to the unchecked flood of sensory inputs, the three-year-old would remain a child for the rest of their lives unless Prakriti took proper care to restrict the synaptic network to a reasonable number of tightly weaved connections. He would never mature into a capable adult since he was unable to interpret or value his surroundings. A person with a stunted mind would never be able to form a personality, a choice, a judgement, a preference, or anything else. This may be regarded as the third element that triggered nature's intervention and resulted in the neural network being cut in half.

To put it plainly, the natural law is hefty! Sir, what steps are being made to strengthen the neural network? Your close network links are strengthened by the union of nature and nurture. At the same time, billions of additional useless connections are also disconnected.

Here, it's critical to understand that our talents are distinctive. It will stick in both of our minds. I wonder why other people feel, think, or behave in ways that are different from how I do, not realising that my own unique thought, feeling, and behaviour patterns may not be those of others.

# How Does The Brain Generate Abilities?

The trainer asserted that our brains first expand more quickly than other organs before starting to contract with ageing. The relationship between IQ and brain size is quite fascinating to think about.

As the scientific exposition got going, the class was paying attention. The first brain nerve cell arises in the embryo around 42 days. It's called a "neuron." Then, 9500 new neurons are created per second as a result of this exponential growth. There are 100 billion neurons in the world 120 days after the first neuron is produced.Wow! Who is able to provide an answer to the query, "What is the value of a billion?" In order to accommodate everyone in the group, the teacher adjusted the inquiry's topic.

What is a billion if one million is ten lakh? Anandavardhan asserted that "a billion is a million times a million." It is one hundred crore in the US. It signifies one lakh crore in English.

The foetus contains 100 billion neurons at 162 days, and this amount does not increase. No matter how old they get, they always have the same birth number.

It doesn't matter that there aren't many neurons. Astonishing changes in the baby's brain begin to occur just sixty days before birth. The 100 billion nerve cells, which were previously dispersed and disconnected, are now beginning to connect.

The relevant question is, "How does it happen?" Axons, which resemble long, finger-like nerve fibres, connect neurons to one another while synapses, also known as docking sites, join neurons together. I believe you ought to elaborate on this a bit more, sir.

And I'll go into further detail. Neurons are the foundation of all nervous system functions. Axons and dendrites are the two basic types of extensions that all neurons have, despite the fact that there are numerous different types of neurons. Axons, which are long, finger-like nerve fibres, and dendrites, which are short branching projects from the cell body, allow neurons to connect with one another.

The actual sites of neuronal communication are 'docking points' (synapses) on the dendrites, where axons from other cells connect. The majority of nerve cells only contain one axon, despite the fact that many of them have many dendrites and docking sites. Dendrites receive the impulses that are sent by axons.

"What are these signals?" you enquire. "A signal is an electrical charge wave that travels from the cell body to the axon. Each neuron functions as a little computer, comparing and weighing the information from other neurons to choose whether and how strongly to "fire" and relay the signal. It is noteworthy that neurons frequently choose information that comes from other neurons who have a "track record" of giving out "reliable" information.

Up to one lakh neurons can send signals to a single neuron. After analysing the data, it will decide which signals to pay attention to and which to disregard. It is amazing how a signal can travel through a massive network of cells, activate the brain, and then represent an idea, a feeling, or a perception together with the behaviour that results.

"Marvellous. Remya remarked, "And we are blissfully oblivious of all these astute judgments that our brain cells are making every second. Remya was speechless from shock.

The instructor said, "Really, that's how the Creator planned and designed the super computer called the brain." It is important to keep in mind that our brain continuously forms new neural connections, changes the strength of existing ones, and adds and deletes connections between neurons. Experience may alter a synapse's capacity, personality, or docking point.

We don't have the knowledge to fully comprehend how the brain functions. It suffices to know that the correct connections between neurons affect our behaviour. In other words, your synapses, which are essentially what cause your skills, are the patterns of recurrent thinking, feeling, or activity.

Neurons are connected by axons, which begin to form sixty days before the baby is born. This process continues throughout the infant's early years of life until the child is three years old. Each of the 100 billion neurons will have developed 15,000 synaptic connections with other nerve cells by the end of the third year. You will create a pattern and a map for your skills over the Book of your life by doing this.

The understudied subject of talent development was being discussed by the entire class, who were all busy taking notes.

# The Destructive Cycle Of Nature

"All right, listen closely while I say more. Then the brain experiences an unanticipated event. That will appear like a strange 12-year annihilation process. The great bulk of the tightly braided neuronal filaments will go unnoticed by nature. You will inevitably develop the habit of ignoring many synaptic connections in your brain as a youngster and adolescent. What will happen to these unused connections? With time, they will deteriorate, break, and wear out.

After the age of three, a portion of the child's brain network will begin to be damaged, erased, and destroyed. A youngster will lose billions upon billions of the delicately woven brain connections between the ages of four and fifteen. Half of the brain network, which began to emerge in the seventh month of pregnancy and continued through the fourth year of life, will have been irreparably damaged by the time the teen awakens to celebrate his sixteenth birthday.

Do you mean damaged past recovery, sir? There is no question in my mind. After that, no more synapses will form?

The brain will still have some of its youthful elasticity after the age of 15, Of course. For instance, a new synaptic connection will form in your brain whenever you learn something new or master a new ability. It will depend on how you handle particular partial impairments, like losing a leg, how you weave new connections. However, the organisation of the brain network typically remains the same after the age of 15. Looks ridiculous, sir. Why does nature act in such an odd way? Why should it let the carefully thought-out networking continue for more than three years before carelessly throwing away half of it? Sandeep asked.

"Let me share with you a fascinating piece of natural history. Nature was known to early Sankhya philosophers as "Prakriti" and "Avyakta," which is a more accurate phrase. This category includes both non-manifested and undifferentiated things. The human brain, one of nature's enigmatic works of art, contains true avyakta. The Shvetashevatara Upanishad claims that Prakriti is once again used to construct the idea of "Maya." The brain also causes the "maya" of prakriti to manifest. Swami Vivekananda believed that nature is God in a scientific sense. When referring to ignorance or a lack of information, the word "nescience" is used. Every name and shape we give things is a fabrication that shows how ignorant we are.

This answer, which will once again serve as a demonstration of our ignorance, will not be pleasing to us simple people who seek logic and reason in everything, in keeping with Vivekananda's concept of "less is more," which is in line with the maxim "less is more." Please be mindful that our brain can only process so much information at once. I'll soon provide you with a stronger, more convincing defence of the wide brain network fading. Kindly wait.

It's crucial to understand that modern parents who yearn after the newest technology in the hope that using it will make their children wiser and smarter are living in a fool's paradise. One cannot get smarter or more intelligent by increasing the number of synaptic connections in their brain. Instead of solely being based on numerical data, creativity, productivity, and similar attributes are also influenced by how well brain connections are formed and used.

But, Sir, how can you maximise and enhance something that you cannot perceive or name?Right now, Sandeep, the Prakriti must be delighted to hear your query. By deleting 50% of the synaptic connections that each of the 100 billion neurons make at a pace of 15,000 connections every second, nature is preventing these problems. so that we can focus on a smaller group of individuals in order to aid and assist the largest number of individuals. Consider this to be one of the causes of Mother Nature's peculiar behaviour in deleting so many connections.

Please keep in mind that there is plenty that a child may learn about the outside world and that nature was kind enough to create so many connections in the first place. Only the child, though, actually executes it. Just take it all in without trying to understand it.

Why is the child only able to absorb things? Why is it unable to interpret what it sees?The youngster is bewildered and overwhelmed by the onslaught of signals from all directions because the child's brain has a big number of synaptic connections, which leads to the child's brain having a large number of synaptic connections. The infant will be inattentive in the midst of the overflowing messages in its brain unless and until a sizable percentage of these signals are refused admission into the mind. Nature will help break up a lot of unnecessary relationships during the next twelve years. The second plausible explanation for Prakriti's peculiar "behaviour" may be related to this.

I agree, but please explain how it helps to create the necessary connections in the brain. When a young child has an early ability for singing, dancing, painting, drawing, etc., is that not a skill? Where does it come from? from the most potent synapses. Similar to this, the strength of a child's synaptic connections can be inferred from the child's natural cognitive, mood, or behaviour patterns, such as their attention to detail, foresight, aptitude for planning, etc. These attitudes and behaviours will strengthen the underlying network connections when they are reinforced both internally and outwardly when they are encouraged and frequently exposed to supportive circumstances.

It might be something like this: The 'birth presents' the creator has given you resemble wrapped presents, much like the usual gifts we give or receive. God will keep providing you with more and more of these wonderful things as soon as you open the birth present packages He gave you and begin using them in your everyday life. When you encourage your child to express talent in singing or drawing, the girl steadily improves, becomes an expert, and is labelled "gifted." This is a signal that the grateful God has been bestowing her with "bonus gifts."

"Sir, what will happen to the network's idle connections?"

These will ultimately die. If a knife is left unused in a kitchen corner for a few months, what will happen to it? Will it not rust and become useless?

But given that nature is not allowed to interfere with the network and the brain is left to function naturally, is it not conceivable that some of the weak network connections could afterwards become stronger in parallel with the preponderant ones, leading to the formation of a genius? The effects would be terrible, my love, even though it's good to use your imagination.

The three-year-old would stay a child for the rest of their lives due to the unrestrained flood of sensory inputs unless Prakriti took sufficient care to limit the synaptic network to a fair number of tightly braided connections. He was unable to comprehend or appreciate his environment, which meant that he would never develop into a competent adult. A person with a stunted intellect is incapable of developing a personality, making decisions, making judgments, forming preferences, or doing anything else. This may be viewed as the third factor that brought about nature's intervention and split the neural network in half.

The natural law is substantial, to put it simply! What efforts are being made, sir, to fortify the neural network?

The fusion of nature and nurture strengthens your close network connections. Hundreds of billions more pointless connections are also cut off at the same time.

Here, it's important to recognize that our talents are unique. Both of us will keep it in mind. I don't realise that my own distinctive thought, feeling, and behaviour patterns may not be those of others, therefore I often wonder why other people feel, think, or act in ways that are different from how I do.

# Parents Ought To Comprehend

People perceive things differently depending on who they are from how we do. But reality still differs from what people perceive it to be. So what varies is personal perspectives. In front of my eyes, I construct my reality. likewise for you. The neuronal network in my brain determines what I see. That also applies to you. Sir, the picture is coming into focus. Despite everyone's best efforts, people are unable to engage effectively due to their disparate frames of reference. They are to blame for this because of their own neural networks. Their varied synaptic connections can be used to explain their wide range of emotions, mental patterns, behaviours, etc. No way, right?

Supriya, I agree with you. Your imagined world has an impact on how you speak. Your companion is able to hear all you say but cannot see what you are seeing. A cheerful person was once questioned about his source of optimism. He claimed that it is easy. You should be grateful that a glass of water is half full when you see it rather than mourning the fact that the upper half is only half full.

It is axiomatic in nature. But numerous studies have discovered that happiness is largely a lifelong personality feature. These individuals are upbeat and like to look on the bright side of everything. The inclination to see the glass as half-full is not something they select; rather, it is an ingrained trait. It is pointless to persuade people who don't have this personality feature to be positive and see the world as half full. It is useless, like encouraging someone to get taller.

Self-help books are widely read and in high demand, sir. It would be intriguing to learn how many of the books' dedicated readers have actually benefited from their research.Supriya, it's a mixed bag. Naturally, one may contend that those who have a predisposition to reflect on and develop the qualities and traits they see in themselves will not profit from the advice and suggestions offered in self-help books. But in the end, everything comes down to making an effort and being persistent. No one can alter the behaviour of another person unless they are equally willing and ready to alter their own. The second important question is: Do you have the skills, personality qualities, and other resources necessary to effect change? The equivalent of a different strategy would be to tell someone to "add two inches to their height."

One must possess the required skills for sustained and enduring changes in one's feelings, ideas, or behaviours. 100 billion neurons, which controlled the Book of your and my existence from the moment we were conceived in the womb, are in charge of that.

If people understood the singularity underlying the repeated patterns of ideas, feelings, or behaviours from the right perspective, wouldn't the majority of conflict and misunderstandings in interpersonal relationships be eliminated? Remya enquired.

In addition, smart parents who are aware of how skills interact with one another will avoid pressuring their children to achieve their own objectives, saving both them and their children from embarrassment and trouble.

The teacher remarked, "Both of you have made accurate observations."Parental indoctrinations that don't include the children's abilities and capabilities are just as useless as trying to describe a certain hue to a colour-blind person. A great author once noted that when you squeeze an orange, only orange juice and not apple juice will come out. Period.

Everybody, not just the parents, ought to be aware of this. These skills are necessary for administrators and business managers alike. When managers can identify the strengths and weaknesses of their team members and use them to their greatest advantage, they grow into effective leaders. But, sir, how do you do it? identifying a person's skills or strengths?"

# Recognizing Talent

Jaleel, there are numerous tactics. Like a flower, some skills will blossom on their own. Please keep in mind the examples of singing, dancing, and painting. When you do a task much more quickly than other people, occasionally even effectively skipping some intermediary stages, without a hitch, and usually with added value, this is a sign that you are applying expertise in your work. Strong indicators of strength include adding value in particular and leaving out specific task phases.

Subject area expert Marcus Buckingham shares some advice on how to identify one's skills. Let's investigate these. One theory is that the best predictors of your abilities are likely your top-of-mind reactions to particular circumstances or stimuli. Imagine that one of your employees called you first thing in the morning to ask for permission to call in sick because his youngster was feeling under the weather. What would be your first reaction to that? Have you thought of anything to help the sick child? can leave people wondering, "What happened to him?" and "Was he taken to the hospital?" If so, it is proof that you possess a great sense of empathy. However, if you were a competent manager and planner, your top priority would be finding a replacement for the staff member and making arrangements for his absence from the office as soon as you learned of his request for leave. Your most prominent talent is "Arranger."

Early on, some children can be recognized to show intense desires for particular things, which may be a sign of developing talents. When he was thirteen years old, Picasso enrolled in an adult arts school. When Mozart was twelve years old, he composed his first symphony.

These rights belong to all people, not just famous ones. It's usual for kids to be drawn to certain hobbies and love participating in them while finding other activities repellent. It is obvious that Tony has an analytical mind and engineering skills when he sits in a corner of the home, engrossed in his favourite activity of disassembling and reassembling his toy cars or other equipment while his siblings and friends are playing a game outside.

The strong synaptic connections in the brain cause childhood passions. Yearnings will still nag despite all limitations, repressions, and unfavourable conditions since the natural forces of nature have immense power. Instead of striving to turn every young Tomy into a doctor or scientist, intuitive parents pay attention to these sparks in their children.

Rapid learning is another indication of brilliance in the making. Take it for granted that your parents are not noticing your early desire cues enough. The vibrant Nature will resume its strategies later in your life, but this time you will be able to witness them firsthand. You might make the decision to attempt something new, have an epiphany about it, and learn it so swiftly that you master it immediately.

One of the young Picasso's contemporaries was Henri Matisse. He was a weak man who supported himself by working as a legal assistant. He was ill and miserable the majority of the time. When Matisse was recovering in bed after contracting the flu once more, his mother reportedly gave him a box of paint. Even though the mother was certain her dejected son had never picked up a brush before, she was anxiously trying to find something to cheer up her hopeless son. The paintbox also proved to be useful.

To put it plainly, the rest is history. The direction and Book of Matisse's life changed significantly. He had a surge of energy that made him feel liberated and as though he had just discovered light. He devoured a how-to book before beginning to cram as much painting and drawing as possible into his days. Four years later, Matisse had his own formal education and was enrolled at the most famous art school in Paris, where he was studying under a well-known professor.

Rapid learning is one characteristic that is shared. The fundamental problem is that it might be habitually disregarded or overlooked. People with exceptional talent may exist in every profession, but they may not always receive the recognition they merit.

Lal said, "Sir," I have a colleague at our workplace. a tech-savvy individual with a below-average IQ. He is constantly in high demand across our network of locations to address any systemic concerns and to launch new projects as they are put forth.

Anandavardhan continued, "Some of us must also be familiar with such occurrences. "When you start a new job or relocate to a different office and are given unexpected tasks, you initially approach a challenge with tremendous anxiety and mistrust. When you start working, though, your mind starts to suddenly light up, you get more confident, you start moving faster, you might even skip one or two stages without taking any risks, and you do the duties with style and ease. You never make clumsy, novice movements. You can even quickly surpass your elders and become known as a rising star within the organisation if you perform well.

The lesson here is that it may indicate that you have hidden skills at work if you are able to pick up a skill more quickly and proficiently than others, thus it is important to follow up on leads like these. They might be the start of the development of matching skills.

Your degree of job happiness is another indicator of talent. Your love for something is evident when you like doing it and feel so satisfied afterward that you eagerly look forward to doing it again. Any passion for one's job comes mostly from one's talent.

Confucius is credited as saying, "If you find a profession you love, you'll never have to work a day in your life," roughly 2500 years ago, according to Remya. "Good. Remya, how do you explain that?

She claimed that if you can find a line of employment that allows you to put your skills to use and something you are passionate about, you won't ever feel like you are "working," and the outcomes would give you a great deal of satisfaction.Well said. A driven worker could become so thrilled that he loses his sense of direction. The instructor said, "Enthusiasm means 'God within.'"

"You claimed, sir, that unlike knowledge and skill, which can both be gained via teaching or catching, abilities cannot be acquired from outside sources. How, then, can you claim, presumably with that objective, that your spiritual organisation has the authority to influence and promote talent development? Sandeep kept at it.

"OK. Excellent point, Sandeep. Let's briefly discuss the epic "Mahabharata" before we respond. A wise sage and King Janaka's spiritual adviser, Ashtavakra, is profiled in the "Vanaparava" section of the poem. The story of Kahodaka, his wife Sujatha, and Sujatha's father Uddhalaka was then told by Anandavardhan.

Sandeep questioned the story after hearing it and deemed it absurd. He investigated if a foetus growing inside a woman's womb could hear, comprehend, and respond to a mantra shouted outside.

# Pregnancy's Seventh Month And The Appearance Of Talent

"I believe our medical student Supriya can resolve Sandeep's problems. Just give us an overview of the foetal development starting in the seventh month of pregnancy, Supriya.OK, Sir. Between 25 and 28 weeks, the seventh month of pregnancy is considered to exist. I'll be gone week after week.

During the 25th week, the foetus's nervous system and brain both rapidly develop. This week, the lungs begin to develop, and the hearing power reaches its peak. The newborn begins dreaming while sleeping off when the baby's sleep-wake cycles become more evident. Now that she can cry, she can also react to various sounds, discomfort, and light. In the 25th week of pregnancy, she is still able to react to external noises.

She begins opening and closing her eyes as the eyelids and brows begin to form. The newborn begins to blink, move in distinct ways, and recognize various noises as her brain cells grow, consciousness, and perception advance. The baby's sense organs become active as her brain develops more swiftly, and she also picks up an increasing variety of skills.

Foetal development peaks in weeks 26 and 27, when hearing and the capacity to react to various noises become more acute and differentiated. The baby practises swift eye opening and closure during the 27th week, suckles thumbs and other fingers, begins to develop sensory skills, and concentrates on visual talents. She begins to pay close attention to the many distinct types and ranges of noises emanating from the mother's external body.

A baby can distinguish between light and dark in the final week of the seventh month. She'll begin swallowing and her blinking will quicken. She can now distinguish her mother's voice from the others and respond to it. As a result, it's typically advised that communication between the mother, father, and other parties start during the seventh month of pregnancy.

During this time, stay away from loud noises that will scare the infant, such as inhaling fireworks, any hard object falling to the ground, etc. Such impulses should also be managed because a newborn has stronger and more acute sensitivity to things like light, pain, etc. The Supriya narrative came to an end.

I'm grateful, Supriya. Hope Sandeep is now persuaded that Ashtavakra's account is supported by the scientific data. Abhimanyu, the son of Arjuna and Subhadra, is another hero in the Mahabharata. He used the information he gained about the Kauravas' incredibly intricate, multi-layered, and specialised combat strategy known as "Chakravyuh" while he was still inside the mother to use his talent to gain entrance inside the Kauravas' creation on the battlefield of Kurukshetra.

When does the spirit first enter the body? The majority of people are already incredibly unaware of it, but the seventh month of pregnancy will see a huge change in foetal growth. Saying "Sir, what is that?" As the spirit or soul enters the fetus's body during the seventh month of pregnancy, this is a vital time.What? How long is the foetus still alive?

Until that point, the foetus is still alive. Supriya made a number of points, all of which were incorrect. This means that "jivatma," a component of the universal spirit, will continue to reside there as long as the fetus's body survives.

"My Guru claims that it is wrong to state that I am Brahman," Malathi continued, "seeing that 'Aham Brahmasmi,' which is Sanskrit for 'I am Brahman,' has been a saying since the time of the Vedas. It has the same impact as saying, "This is the ocean," after scooping up some ocean water. You are not the Brahman; you are merely a component of it. The cosmic soul is much larger than the indwelling spirit, Jivatma, that resides within you and me.

The soul locates a location in space-time, according to Deepak Chopra, and broadcasts or telecasts through the body. My physique is simply the physical expression of my spirit, to put it simply. It is said that the soul is transcendent. According to Deepak, the term "jivatama" refers to the localised manifestation of the omnipresent and omniscient soul.

The spiritual master's claim that "Aham Brahmasmi" is erroneous is supported by this scientific viewpoint. Supraja agreed with Malathi's claim that the transcendent is not limited by either space or time.

The jivatma enters the foetal body in the seventh month of pregnancy, according to the Malayalam encyclopaedia "Puranik Encyclopedia" by Vettom Mani, commented Remya. The trainer concurred, "It's in there." It is difficult to understand that the mother carries a spiritless foetus in her womb for more than two thirds of the pregnancy. Thomas kept having his doubts.

Thomas, this knowledge is not untrue just because few people are aware of it. Readers will never forget the amazing chariot comparison used in the "Kathopanishad". Even the iconic pictures of the chariot, horses, bridle, and charioteer from the Bhagavad Gita are thought to have been inspired by this Upanishad.

The human body is the "Kada's" chariot. The brain is the charioteer. The brain is the charioteer, and the mind is the reins. The five senses, represented by the horses, are those that seek out the positive aspects of life.

You couldn't understand how or why, up until the seventh month of pregnancy, the foetus continues to exist without a soul. Let me use an example from the Kathopanishad to clarify everything.

We recognize that the chariot or carriage won't carry a passenger until it is prepared for the trip ahead. The horses must be properly bridled and throat-latched before the charioteer may assume his position and take over command of the animals. These actions cannot be performed in reverse, therefore the passenger must board the carriage before it can be set up for the voyage.

Similar to this, the foetal body, which functions as the chariot in this instance, is made ready and fit to begin the life trip, with the charioteer (intellect), the horses (the five sense-organs), and the reins (mind) all functionally in place. Only the jivatma, the vehicle's traveller, will thereafter manifest and take a seat atop the chariot after that.

It should be observed that until the spirit has entered the body, the expanding sense organs, mind, and intellect cannot accept inputs and respond appropriately. Or, to put it another way, the soul will only enter the body and activate these faculties when they are ready to carry out their designated tasks.

What use does the soul serve in the body, sir? "As everyone is aware, the accumulated karmic weight is a vital factor in the jivatma's body's endowment. Because its goal is to discharge all the karma it has accumulated over the Book of previous lives, the soul needs a body. The soul continues to accrue new karmas throughout this incarnation in addition to carrying over some of the old ones, so the jivatma's journeys through the cycle of births and deaths of the bodies it occupies will continue.

Permit me to go into further detail about this. A man is regarded as having passed away when he finally exhales and is unable to breathe in again. This indicates that the journey in the now existing existence is over and the jivatma, or soul, has left the body. The deceased spirit must also wait in time and space until the right moment to enter a suitable foetal body. We refer to the first breath a newborn takes after delivery as "being born." As a result, the initial intake signifies birth, and the last expiration depicts death. What is lost at the end of one life is gained back in another. Then, in order to dissipate the karmic weight it holds, the lifeless jivatma continues on its trip. This loop keeps going. This is life as we know it, to put it briefly.

"Sir, we are aware of the jiva, or life force, that resides within us. What is the evidence that a soul exists? But isn't the idea of the soul, or jivatma, too abstract to understand? Is there evidence to support its existence? Jaleel was the one who asked the query.

The earth should be flat and the sun should rise in the east and set in the west in the sea if what can be seen with the unaided eye alone is the truth, Jaleel.

But scientists are in agreement about the sun and the planet. I'd like to know whether there is any evidence that a spirit is here.We both find logic and mathematical problems to be quite enjoyable, Jaleel. Even so, it is true that God's truths begin when human reason and understanding collapse and cease to be restless rumblings. Only after science has achieved its pinnacle or reached a dead end can the mysteries of spirituality begin to be understood.

The wise advise against bowing to the five senses' dominance. There are two main reasons why our senses can fool us. One is that the construction of the sense organs prevents them from being limited to external signals and stimuli. Second, as Swami Vivekananda noted, "we have been taught to pay attention only to the things external, and never to the internal, from our childhood onward." As a result, the majority of us are almost incapable of seeing internal mechanisms.

You have to look within if you want to understand the soul since it resides there. The two bodies are impenetrable, so the sense organs cannot peek into them. Two dead bodies? Who exactly are the two bodies?

Each of us has both intrusive and subtle body types. Earth, water, fire, air, and ether are the five elements that make up the outer or gross body. The mind, intellect, and ego are components of the subtle body. Even though they are not apparent to unaided sight, none of the three subtle bodily parts will be denied existence.

Both the gross and subtle bodies conceal the soul, also known as the jivatma, which is invisible to the sense organs.

Define death. The disgusting body is the only thing being destroyed. The mysterious body still exists. In addition, after the death of the gross body, the subtle body directs the jivatma to a new, suitable gross body in due Book. The kind of gross body a jiva forms depends on its characteristics, flaws, and "bhagya".

Here is a Chandogya Upanishad tale that demonstrates the existence of a soul. When Svethakethu was about Ashtavakra's age, he went to Ashtavakra's grandfather, Aaruni, also known as Uddhalaka, and asked particularly about the presence of ghosts. He was instructed to bring a banyan tree fruit by his father, a wonderful teacher. Aaruni begged him to open it for her when he brought one.

A few small seeds were later discovered inside the apple by the young boy. When he opened one of the seeds after being asked again, surprise, surprise, nothing was inside! The father told him that one day that little seed would sprout into a big banyan tree. Similar to how the source of everything that can be seen is our soul, a weak and unseen power that is within us. The boy was persuaded once Aaruni said, "That spiritual force controls everything in you and me."

The instructor opened his laptop and switched on the projector. On the screen behind him, there was a slide. If all you can see is what the light discloses and all you can hear is what the sound proclaims, it was stated that you are actually neither seeing nor hearing. Khalil and Gibran

"Sir, once a specific type of wood was attrited to create fire for sacrificial rituals (yaga). Early man used to make fire by attrition of dry twigs before the invention of the match box. Which implies that even if there was fire in the wood or twig, it was concealed until it was called upon. Malathi agreed with the details shown on the screen.going back to the instant the spirit entered the foetal body. Anandavardhan drew attention to the fact that the Garbha Upanishad describes the soul's fusion with the body as occurring during the seventh month of pregnancy.

Is there another Upanishad that is comparable?

Not familiar? Names like Kadopanishad, Ishopanishad, Mandukya, etc. are well known to us. The seventeenth of the 108 Upanishads in the current collection is the Garbha Upanishad. The Krishna Yajurveda contains it. The verse is as follows: Jeevan Samyuktha Bhavathi, Sarvasampoorno Bhavathi, and Ashtame Maase, By the eighth month, when the foetus enters the jeevatma, it is fully matured.

Why are we unable to recall our previous lives? What does that mean, sir? Complete in every way by the eighth month. Another remarkable aspect of a baby's prenatal development that the general public is mostly unaware of is that. The foetal soul can meditate, recall its previous existence, experience "Om," and begin to have an intuitive sense of right and wrong during the eighth month. The foetus recalls both its positive and negative karma during the final weeks of development.

Does this imply that a newborn will have memories of the past?

"No. The newborn experiences severe trauma and distress during the "shunting out" process from the uterus. The baby forgets its former births and the good and evil deeds of earlier lifetimes because it is engulfed by an all-pervading movement called "maya" as it enters the birth canal and is dragged out against its will. Additionally, it's thought that touching the vagina and breathing in fresh air from the outside can completely erase the newborn's recollection.

Contrary to spontaneous deliveries, Caesarean births constitute the majority of births conducted today. Then, will such young kids be able to remember their previous births? No. Again, even if there isn't a natural shunting out, the baby will be stressed by the abrupt handling inside the uterus, and the quick exposure to air will make this stress worse. The baby will therefore be born in both cases with no memory of the past. Play a game called "maya," if you will.

# One Of A Kind Prenatal Spiritual Intervention

Let's now talk about the talent development initiatives the Ashram is implementing. It is, as I have already indicated, a prenatal spiritual intervention to adorn the jiva of the unborn with the grace and majesty of the Guru while purging it of any potential vices. It is referred to as "jivasuddhi" or "jiva karma" (purificatory rite) in the spiritual jargon of the ashram.Sir, when will it be finished?

Because it targets the jivatma, which the foetus lacks before the seventh month of pregnancy, treatment must take place during that time. The Guru-apparent provides the couple with the required instructions and a special "sankalpa" (invocative focused prayer) when they go to the Ashram. They participate in each and every (daily) "aaradhana" (worship) in the prayer hall, sit in sankalpa (meditation posture) at the designated mandir in front of the form of the Guru, and offer their own sankalpa prayer interspersed with the Ashram's akhandanamajapa" (the customary prayer) and the regular sankalpa" (given to all the devotees). Flowers and leaves of holy basil are utilised in the offerings.

Why was this religious ceremony specifically chosen for the seventh month? Why is it not carried out immediately once a pregnancy is known to be present? Can Malathi answer?" inquired the trainer.

Malathi pondered for a moment before saying, "The child in the womb should be able to hear and understand the prayers and sankalpa supplied by the parents. Around the seventh month of pregnancy, when the fetus's hearing ability becomes apparent, the other four sense organs also start to develop. We are informed that throughout pregnancy, both Abhimanyu and Ashtavakra could hear and take in external stimuli.

The physiological processes enable the growing foetus to react to outside stimuli because of the beneficent spirit's existence within the body. As a result, the seventh month of pregnancy should be used for the jivasuddhi karma.OK. As a medical student, how would you, Supriya, explain the significance of this activity at this time? Anandavardhan, I'm enquiring.

We now know that each of the 100 billion neurons in the brain forms synaptic connections with other nerve cells via 15,000 axons, enabling inter-se communication. Supriya got to her feet and said. This lays the foundation for the child's future personality, especially in terms of their ability, prowess, attitude, and other traits. Of course, now is the time to pray for the blessings of the Almighty to aid in the development of the unborn child's talents and character.

"OK. Malathi and Supriya, thank you. I'm hopeful that the revised versions have improved everyone's learning. Let me now add some dotted lines to the plot and fill them in as well. said the trainer.

"As we have learned, synaptic connections are the pathways via which the impulses of human thoughts, feelings, and behaviours flow and eventually determine a person's fate. Each neuron constructs 15,000 'bridges'. There are 100 billion of them, and they all act in this way. What neurons connect with what others, then? The answer to this issue becomes more significant because it will ultimately determine what kind of character or strength is developed in the person. As an illustration, consider the talent "XYZ" that is created when neuron "B" joins neuron "A". If neuron "A" communicates with nerve cell "C," not "B," the ensuing talent will be "PQR," not "XYZ."

Assume that XYZ represents the skill "empathy." Sandeep will exhibit tremendous empathy when interacting with others if neuron 'A' and neuron 'B' are synaptically coupled. In contrast, if Sandeep's A synapses with C, he might acquire great analytical skills or a keen sense of curiosity but not empathy. Think of Sandeep, the analyst, as a bank employee who must complete a customer care training Book. Sandeep will learn during the Book how important it is to put oneself in the customer's shoes, comprehend his unique wants, and meet them. He will be aware of how important empathy is to giving great customer service.

Imagine that after the training, Sandeep returns to his bank branch and is met by a client who is dissatisfied with the branch's subpar service since he suffered financial loss as a result. Or perhaps he gets a request for a longer grace period to repay an Agricultural Cash Credit from a different client whose crops didn't work out. What will occur? He will be able to hear what these two clients are saying, but he won't be able to understand what they are thinking or feeling.

He will not and cannot take off his own shoes in order to place himself in the shoes of these constituents, hence he will not and cannot do so. It wasn't done intentionally. Due to the way he thinks, he will likely examine the scenario in a way that benefits the bank rather than the clients. because he lacks empathy as a talent.

For a number of reasons, including (i) the physiological changes in the body and mind, especially the fully developed hearing system, (ii) the soul (jivatma) joining the life force and enhancing the sensory abilities, and (iii) the formation of synaptic connections in the brain that determine the talents in the new one, the seventh month of pregnancy is an important milestone in both prenatal and postnatal life. Naturally, during this month, the Ashram completes the Jivasuddhi Karma.

Malathi grinned, "Sir, I might now have the added advantage of finishing a difficult task. The trainer turned his head to look at her with interest.

She noted that it "always used to catch my eye with appreciating astonishment in the Ashram " how little children could recite the lengthy, intricate, akhanda nama mantra with such ease and clarity. My current theory is that these lyrics were passed down to them by their moms, who carried their children about on their arms, waists, or laps while they strolled and worshipped in the Ashram. I now see that, like Ashtavakra and Abhimanyu, their learning started far earlier than delivery, in the seventh month of pregnancy. It shouldn't come as a surprise that even the Sanskrit terms of the "Guru Gita " and genuflexion and prostration before the Guru come naturally and easily to them.

Anandavardhan went on, nodding in accord, "There is one more significant importance for the said spiritual intervention." Can someone try their hand at it?

Supriya put up her hand. "Sir, it is widely known that the most potent synaptic connections in the brain promote the development of genius. I thus assume that the purpose of the particular sankalpas and prayers is to strengthen these ties in order for the kid to be blessed at birth.You're right. Sandeep seemed to be eager to talk. Sandeep, please stand up.Between the ages of four and fifteen, the child's brain often neglects, weakens, and eventually loses billions of network connections. There's a chance that some of these injured synapses still had untapped potential for growth that, given the appropriate conditions, might even have fructified. The spiritual intervention suggested here may be an appeal to the Almighty to prevent the potential connections that would eventually form from disintegrating in the future and to allow them to continue in a fruitful way.Sandeep halted.

You're absolutely right, Sandeep. I value your thoughtful remarks. In the event that two or three requirements are met, children can develop exceptionally good talents. One is that a certain neuron needs to connect to an appropriate neighbouring neuron. The newly generated synapse also needs to be robust and long-lasting. The third component is the 'bhagya' of the jivatma. The Ashram's spiritual practices are intended to cleanse the jivatma of its vices and request God's grace in accordance with the credentials attained in past lives. Again, the punya and bhagya of the receiving jivatma are involved in this. My dear friends, today has come to an end.

Personal power is the culmination of talent, skill, and knowledge. For the best results, all three elements must be present. Knowledge can either be acquired through learning or catching, as well as through experiences.

The capacity to carry out specific duties successfully and methodically is referred to as a skill. It is refined via persistence and exercise. There is innate talent. is not something that can be learned or trained for, but repetition can make it stronger.

A skill is the capacity to consistently repeat thinking, emotion, or behaviour patterns in one's day-to-day activities. The synapses in the brain are where the 100 billion neurons dock and form the 15,000 connections with other nerve cells. The growth of abilities is facilitated by these synaptic connections.

Beginning in the seventh month of pregnancy and continuing until the third year of life, synapse development. Around fifty percent of the connections formed up to the third year will be weakened, damaged, and effaced between the fourth and fifteenth years due to involuntary neglect and disuse.

The strongest preserved links activate thinking, emotion, or behaviour patterns, which in turn activate talent. Early, untaught demonstration of special aptitudes and abilities, such as an interest in the arts, is one sign of intrinsic talent. Additional signs of pulsing abilities are spontaneous emotions, responses to certain situations, yearnings in the early stages of life, rapid learning, and contentment with the task at hand.

In an Ashram established by a recognized teacher, a special spiritual practice is practised in order to support the development of the gifts during the foetus stage. During the seventh month of pregnancy, the foetal body goes through significant physiological changes that include the development of the foetal brain, functional lungs, an advanced hearing and visual system, cognition, and the mind.

The physiological systems of the foetal body are activated by the union of the foetal body's vital energy and the soul or spirit (jivatma), which occurs in the seventh month of pregnancy.

Beginning in the seventh month, the brain network that builds skills begins to weave. The jivatma's punya and bhagya decide whether the brain network will remain robust over the Book of a lifetime. This increases the significance of spiritual participation at this critical juncture.

By performing the aforementioned technique, you are asking the Almighty to grant the Guru's blessing to the jivatma so that enduring neural connections can be made and potential ones can be protected from the synapses' unavoidable natural degradation.

The outcome of this spiritual endeavour will depend on the jivatma's eligibility, as demonstrated by the punya and bhagya of the soul, as well as how the parents and the unborn child spend their lives, adhering to and abiding by the teachings of the Guru.

# Mind And Matter

I'm quite thirsty. Why don't you see whether there's any nearby water? Nakul climbed a tree and looked around, noticing a number of green spaces close by. He got down, spoke to his brother, took his quiver, and entered the dense undergrowth to find some water.

He made the right assumption. It wasn't far distant either. A beautiful, sizable body of water surrounded by lush vegetation, plants bearing lovely flowers bending down into the waters and enjoying the reflection of their beauty, and birds of different colours squawking and singing from the trees, some of which were swooping down into the water and emerging with a catch of fish.For a while, Nakul was enthralled by the visual feast in front of him.

He then ducked into the pond, knelt down, and drank water with his hands. An unidentified sound frightened him. Child of Pandu, hold on. The land with this pond on it belongs to my family. You cannot harvest water from my pond or drink from it if you don't respond to my inquiries.

Nakul stood up straight and searched the area for the intrusive party. He looked about but found nothing, so he drank the water as he was already very thirsty.

After a lengthy interval, Yudhistar pushed Sahadev to locate Nakul and hastily procure some water. Sahadev was astounded by what he discovered when he finally arrived at the pond and green belt. At the edge of the water, his valiant and cherished brother's body was found. He wept loudly while sitting near the deceased man's body. Sahadev, who was quite worn out, struggled to his feet and made his way to the pond to find some water. He heard the same ghostly voice Nakul had when he bowed to get a glass of water. He also paused for a few while to glance around, stunned by what he perceived. When Sahadev couldn't see anyone on the trees or surrounding the pond, he thought the warning was a delusion and drank some water.

Arjun was left to go in search of the younger children when neither of them came back. The greatest of heroes was horrified when he realised the most terrible disaster awaiting him. How is it even conceivable that? Any kind of toxicity at all? Arjun was really perplexed. He cried hysterically, sitting near to the bodies of his loved ones. He observed that the pond was only a few steps away, and he proceeded cautiously in that direction, his hunger being intense.

Hello, Kunti's son. Don't be careless. Before you can take a drink from my pond, you must respond to my questions.

Arjun was surprised by the sudden instruction. He reacted passionately and furiously, "Validity is not in hiding oneself like a coward and shooting a threat. There is no act of bravery in the terrible loss of the brothers on one side or the mother's and elders' never-ending hunger on the other. If you dare, approach me and challenge me. You will then become familiar with Arjun. The skilled shooter then fired arrows at lightning speed in all directions.

Dhananjay, I won't be injured by your arrows, rang out the peal of thundering laughter. Either respond to my inquiries or avenge your killed buddies.

Arjun disregarded the ethereal words because he wasn't used to obeying commands from others and drank water from the pond instead.

Unaware of the thirsty mother and the two elders, Dharmaputra grew restless and wondered where his siblings were relaxing. He gave Bhima the mission to look into it.

Rebellious Bhima, horrified by what he had unintentionally discovered at the pond, raised his mace and roared loudly, trembling the bush. He yelled obscenities and taunts at a potential adversary, prepared to engage and defeat the foe. Soon after, he wailed uncontrollably while sitting near to the bodies of his loved ones.

Bhima moved to the pond to obtain some water because he was so thirsty. The unbending warrior also disregarded the warning he heard, which resulted in the deaths of his siblings.

Dharmaputra was the last to perish. After being made to leave his mother, the bereaved eldest Pandava set off in search of his brothers and eventually arrived at the pond area. He was so appalled by what he saw that he rushed over to the boys' dead bodies and started crying uncontrollably. All of his hopes for the future were abruptly destroyed all around him!

How all four powerful warriors could be destroyed in a single blow without any signs of an attack, bruises, or wounds puzzled him. Then, weak and thirsty, Yudhishtir hobbled over to the pond and bent down to drink.

Hello, Kunti's son. I am a crane that consumes aquatic plants and fish. I killed your brothers because they refused to listen to me and tried to drink my water before answering my questions. If you give me an answer to my inquiries, you can have the water and your life. Lest you follow your gasping brothers and sisters. Your decision is your own.

Dharmaputra cocked his head toward the voice and then took a straight stance. "Lord, may I know who you really are," he sweetly prayed as he raised his reverently folded palms. I'm confident that a simple crane won't be able to harm my valiant brothers, who are unbeatable even against the devas. It proves you are better than other devas. Please introduce yourself and explain what you're doing. I'm near death, extremely thirsty, and I'm grieving the loss of my brothers. Please have mercy and put an end to this charade, I ask you.

The big wading bird that had been seen suddenly gave way to a colossal and horrifying monstrosity with keen eyes and the glitter of the early sun. It was a yaksha. It started yelling, "Who is carrying Adhitha?" and asking questions. Who are Aditya's supporters? What causes the sun to set? On whom is the light focused?

Dharmaputra folded his hands and started answering the interrogative questions. Brahman carries Athithaya. Adhithya has the support of the Devas. Due to dharma, aditya "sets". Adhithya sathya, or "remains on the truth,"

Questions and responses started to clash one against the other like arrows. Yudhishtir provided explanations for the laws that govern the universe, the secrets and riddles of existence, as well as his sharp insight into the moral conundrums that humans encounter.

"You have correctly addressed all of my questions," the pleased yaksha said in response to Yudhishtir's response. In exchange for your assistance, I'll resurrect one of your brothers. You may only choose one of these.

Yaksha hurled the false offer while intently observing Dharmaputra. Pat was the eldest of the five to answer. "Nakul. Please, bring Nakul back to life.

The yaksha responded, "Bhima and Arjuna must be your pioneers in a possible future war with the Kauravas," appearing shocked by the answer. Why do you choose Nakul over Bhima or the strong Arjun?

The destroyer of dharma shall be destroyed by dharma, Dharmaputra promptly retorted. The same way, Dharma will stand up for its messiah. I'll never give up the dharma. And I perceive that selfishness is violent, while the highest form of dharma is nonviolence. Kunti and Madri are equal to me. Asking for Bhima or Arjun would be violent and egotistical on my part because I am Kunti's son. I made the decision to accompany Madhri ma's son Nakul.

Yaksha was now overjoyed. You clearly place non-violence above worldly possessions, pleasures, and desires, he continued. Therefore, all of your brothers will live again. They actually all did. Dharmaputra expressed the utmost gratitude and humility in his speech. Master, you still haven't identified yourself. Please let me know whether I have any right to know that information.

The deva then said, "I am your father, Dharmadev," revealing his identity. I arrived to check on your adherence to the dharma. You were successful, too. God's blessings are upon you. Let the best and everything just be yours.

# A Personality For Altitude

In the previous class, we discussed skills in great detail. Today, we'll discuss a subject that is equally significant: mindset. Anandavardhan then started teaching about personal growth.

He asserted that all of our words, deeds, and behaviours stem from our attitudes. The saying "Sow a thought, reap a word, sow a word, sow an action, sow an action, sow a habit, sow a habit, sow a character, sow a character, reap a destiny" was added by Sandeep.

"Good," replied the trainer. "Words come first in thinking, then comes action. You can inquire, "Sir, how does a habit form?" "Anything you repeatedly do turns into a habit, which then develops into your character.

Any behaviour that is sustained for twenty-one days without interruption becomes a habit. It takes another 21 days of repetition for it to become ingrained in your way of life.

The lecturer unlocked his laptop and turned on the LCD projector. He looked over the powerpoint slides. A flash of an iceberg appeared on the screen shortly after that. He asked, "What do you see here, and how would you describe it?"

A small bit of the iceberg, which is what it is, can be seen above the water. Lal said that a large portion of it is submerged in water. "Can a human analogy be made?

The class was silent for a split second. Everyone's attention was focused on the iceberg. According to Thomas, a person's abilities are only partially on display in daily life. The remainder is always hidden within him, Anandavardhan chuckled. Although Thomas makes a strong case, I had hoped for a different result. Only 10% of people's brain power, according to behavioural scientists, is actually employed. The famous quote from Sir Oliver Wendel Holmes goes, "What is inside of you is more important than what is outside of you." He also asserted that the bulk of us are hiding our inner melodies as we visit cemeteries. What a terrible circumstance.What causes this, sir? Will people's failure to develop their talents and abilities throughout their lives have no visible cause? Sandeep asked.

"Once a similar issue was brought up to our previous President, APJ Abdul Kalam," the trainer continued. Parents and primary school instructors will have to consider that answer, he retorted. Though inadvertently, these individuals are impairing their kids' hidden abilities and potential.

Sir, how and why?It necessitates a thorough conversation. But since you asked, let me tell you about the circumstances. Since the first publication of Dr. Thomas A. Harris' foundational work in Transactional Analysis (TA) in the 1960s, our comprehension of interpersonal behaviours and relationships has significantly advanced. Why people don't live as effectively as they already know how to was a topic Harris addressed. Four different life positions—for oneself and others—are established by TA.

Remya, a psychology student, answered, "I'll tell that Sir." She was pleased that the subject was becoming increasingly pertinent to her area of specialisation. The instructor granted the go-ahead. You're doing OK, but I'm not. Our health is both poor. I'm okay, but you're not. You and I both are OK. Hello, Remya. The instructor took charge.

One individual, three states, and three ideas. How does this decent business function? Suhra reflected while sitting in the back of the class. I'll be clear. Just keep in mind that Suhra is conversing with a friend. Your friend once advised you to exercise caution because it seemed as though you were acting like a three-year-old in everything you said and did. At that very moment, a "Child" was acting within Suhra. Suhra reiterates, "See, this is too much," to her pal.

You shouldn't have spoken to her in that way. Understand your limitations. A "Parent" in Suhra gave such a response. Another instance was when Suhra appeared to be acting rationally and responsibly in a conversation with a friend. At that point, Suhra's "Adult" was acting inappropriately. In this instance, Suhra, a single person, demonstrates three distinct personality types depending on the circumstance.

This is a skill that can be used by more than simply Suhra, Sujatha, or Sandeep. Each of us possesses the three states of being: child, parent, and adult. It comes from the encounters we have had at various ages or times throughout our lives. Additionally, these experiences and the emotions they elicit are constantly and in-the-moment stored in the brain, where they are repeated in line with one's perception of them in the future. You can exhibit childlike behaviour at times and adult or parental behaviour at other times.

"Sir, is this adult state within a person evolving after he or she reaches adulthood, and the parent state within a person evolving after a person becomes a parent?"

As I said earlier, the assumption of all three internal states—Child, Parent, and Adult—is based on the replay of recordings in the brain. A child not only has the Child state but also the Parent and Adult states since a child's brain begins to record events and stimuli from the outside world when he is young, whether they are offered to him voluntarily or are forced upon him.

Regarding the adult status, you inquired. The kid initially experiences the power of locomotion in the tenth month of life. He is now free to move around and exert control over things as he sees fit, based on his own expertise and unique thoughts, having been set free from his prior position of helplessness. He is now starting to exhibit characteristics of the adult state. The 'thought concept' of life is the origin of adult data recorders.

In contrast, the parent and child data recorders start considerably sooner. The "felt idea" of life, which are the recordings of "internal" events that are the young child's reactions to what he hears and sees around him, is where child data comes from. What we refer to as the "Child" within a person is the "seeing and hearing and feeling and understanding" body of information.

In stark contrast to the thought concept (Adult) and the felt concept (Child), which are represented by the other two data sets, the Parent data represents the "taught concept" of life. A person's first five years of life are distinguished by a considerable collection of exterior events that they observe, as opposed to the child's internal experiences.

In the first five years of existence, "Why?"Because when a person leaves home and begins their education in their fifth year of life, that is when they often experience their social birth. The little child, who is still in preschool, keeps a notebook of all he hears, sees, and experiences from his parents. Each individual has a unique bond with their parents as well as unique early experiences.What his parents did or said before he entered school, sir, will he remember and be impacted by for how long?

It was documented in writing. This suggests that while the action can always be replayed, it cannot ever be undone. Because they are unaltered data that were carefully recorded as they came from the child's own world, the source of all of his identity and security, they have a huge impact on a person's entire life.

Does this imply that all of the parental knowledge that was retained in the child's brain until the age of five was provided by the parents?No. All of a person's parents and other family members have an impact on the "taught" outlook on life. For instance, everything a young child discovers on social media or hears and sees while glued to the TV for hours on end contributes to the lessons they are taught about life.

The young child is forced to accept all of these external events and stimuli as true because he is too small, the others are too big, and he is unable to confront them. And he draws on this vast repository of learned information that the brain's "always-on" recorder stores over the Book of a person's lifetime. That was instructive and intriguing, sir. What about the statistics from adults?

Because the Adult in the person analyses the knowledge in his Parent to determine its relevance and applicability at the time in question before deciding whether to accept or reject it, this idea is known as the thinking concept. The child will undergo the same analysis as the adult to see whether the emotions shown are appropriate for the current circumstance.

Because it holds that content should change in accordance with the circumstance. In other terms, an adult is a computer that processes data. It breaks down inputs into informational building blocks, examines those building blocks, and then saves them according to knowledge. The instructor turned on the projector and displayed a powerpoint slide that described the three aspects of human nature.

Now, Suhra's inquiry is met with the following response: He then addresses his parents by saying, "You're OK," because a child's sense-based understanding of reality leads them to believe that "I'm not OK." Understanding himself and the society he lives in is the first lesson he learns in life. "I'm not OK, you're OK" is the principle that follows in interpersonal interactions. He makes the most predetermined decision he has ever had to make, and it will always stick in his mind. This crucial choice he makes will have an impact on everything he does.

Do you really intend to say that the child will always decide to do that action? No. You have my word that it will last forever. In the tenth month of life, The Adult makes its initial appearance in the child's brain. In light of this new perspective on life, the choice based on the inner child's notion and the lesson learned from their parents may change. After considering the new context and confirming the accuracy of the evidence, the person then comes to a new choice.

Remya mentions three different vantage points on life: "I'm not OK-You're OK," Young children often assume that "I'm not OK-you're not OK" and "I'm OK-you're not OK," which are based on the imagined notion of life. A child will almost certainly identify with and establish themselves in one of these three areas by the end of their second year of life or the beginning of their third year.

Based on his perceptions and experiences during his first year, he is more likely to adopt the perspective of "I'm not OK-You're OK." By the time he is two, he will either go to the second or third life position, or he will stay there permanently. I'm okay, you're okay, and you're not okay are comparable words.

Do you really mean to say that it will change his perspective on life? Supriya enquired. Simply that. Whether or not this desire is conscious, it will manifest in the person's thoughts, feelings, and behaviours as a desire to hold onto the life position that has already been chosen.

The question is, "Can't he change it?" I'm unsure.If he is successful in his steadfast, unyielding efforts to alter his perspective, he can. If it does, he'll swap out "I'm OK-You're OK" for the fourth person.

But, sir, don't these positions change according to the circumstances? "You're OK," "I'm not OK," and "Are we?" to "Are we both OK then?" Malathi posed a wise query. However, topic experts think that such a shift in one's life circumstances after achieving a particular level is rather exceptional. It is of enduring quality. The first three positions, however, are all either held or empty for the same reason.

"What's that, Sir?" was questioned. A stroke can result in both positive and negative observable and intangible effects. All three of the aforementioned positions are non-verbal indicators of the child's feelings, depending on whether or not there was any hugging or fondling when the child was an infant. The young child has drawn these conclusions without any supporting evidence.

Sir, first. During the first year of life, a baby receives a lot of cuddling. How could there be a judgement that I'm not OK and you're OK despite all the love and care that was lavished upon him in abundance?Thomas, I think your question is generally sound. It is true that a child receives the most love, care, and support during the first year of life. In addition, he perceives that they are conveying, "I'm OK." In addition, he claims that, at least according to him, he frequently encounters far more horrible than positive events.

I need an explanation, sir.Sure. I'll be explicit. Because he perceives his parents as being big, smart, and strong, the youngster is better able to tolerate his extreme smallness, helplessness, and dependency on others thanks to his perception of himself. Additionally, he anticipates them to meet all of his wants. He can only evaluate himself based on what these "big others" have to say. He can't reasonably risk insulting them, either. He has learned that he is inferior to the adults on whom he depends in every aspect as a result of the conditions of his existence. He is expressing, "They're OK, I'm not," by doing this.

At the age of 10 months, he discovers the power of movement and begins to exert influence on those around him by using a lot of quick, forceful strokes. His suffering from his parents' critical looks, other body language cues, shifting voice tones, and harsh remarks pales in contrast to the earlier manifestations of love and devotion. To put it simply, he says, "I'm not OK—You're OK."

That makes sense, said Sandeep. A young child hears around 148,000 words and phrases that limit or delay his activities before the age of fifteen. As a young youngster, he is frequently instructed to "don't touch it," "take it," "do it," etc. People frequently admonish young children, "Don't experiment with it or your life," "Does anyone else think the way you do," "Don't waste your life," "What a foolish thing have you done," and "Will you ever do anything properly?"

The child will hear these dire warnings of punishment and restriction 100 times after the initial instance. He or she will then start to think, "others are capable and smart, they're OK," as opposed to, "I'm not OK, I don't know anything, and I am a coward." It is obvious how significant Kalam was. Sir's veiled allusion to the improper teacher mentoring and parenting that was previously mentioned.

Child psychologists contend that categorical criticism from parents and teachers will have a more significant psychological impact on children than any prescriptive language.

Let's look at a few situations where they differ, sir. Statements like "You are a bad boy," "You are a liar," "You don't have the intelligence of your sister," etc. are examples of accusatory or explicit allegations. Children are expected to follow rules when they are told to do things like "always wash your hands before taking food," "don't put toys in your mouth," "arrive at school on time," "always show respect to the elders by getting up from your seat," etc.

It implies that a child's self-awareness has a much greater influence on them than any directives or words. This will also reinforce the presumptive life position that individuals have been developing since they were between the ages of two and three. That assumption suggests that his personality and behaviour will be shaped. Negative comments made by adults regarding children often get swiftly ingrained in their impressionable minds. comparable to fruits and seeds, or plants and plants.

Humans are special in that our bodies and brains always mirror the sensations we audibly express. Additionally, one's words have the power to do more emotional injury than any outside objects. In other words, both the words we speak and the comments spoken about us have an impact on who we are.

Getting the response "Not clear, Sir" will make everything clear. The mind has an impact on every cell in the body. Do you know how many cells there are in a human body? Think about the fact that the brain alone contains 100 billion trillion neurons. Jaleel remembered what they had talked about in the prior lesson. A newborn baby has fifty trillion cells, according to research. One trillion rupees equal one lakh crore. It makes more sense that the human body contains more cells than there are stars in the Milky Way galaxy. Who knows how many of these 50 trillion cells are present in the human brain?

"Sir, I remember reading somewhere that the mind is present in every atom of the body," Sandeep continued. Your viewpoint is becoming more clear.

# Biology Is Influenced By Belief

Anandavardhan asserts that the study's findings demonstrate that nothing has a greater impact on a person's physical appearance than their thoughts. Therefore, we might assert that our thoughts and emotions have an effect on how our bodies are made. Believe it or not, according to Norman Cousins, "belief creates biology."

Is this just relevant to people? Yes. The only animal known to be capable of changing his biology through ideas and emotions is man. Because, as we discovered in the previous lesson, he only possesses self-awareness.

Additionally, he is the only person with a brain system that is conscious of ageing. For example, a lion or tiger that is old and withering away is ignorant of its condition. But we humans are aware of that. As a result, our awareness of ourselves is influenced by our mental health.

"I responded, "Isn't that why AdhiSankara claimed that people age and die when they observe others doing so? Supriya recalled the teacher's advice from the previous lesson.Correct. Experts estimate that only 1% of the yearly changes in your body are brought on by ageing. Ipso facto, it's straightforward to understand how attitudes and beliefs could impact someone's physiology.

However, this fact has a secondary benefit. Ninety-nine percent of your energy and intelligence are unaffected by age, demonstrating that by maintaining optimistic attitudes and beliefs, we can slow down the body's degradation or fading away and delay ageing. The adage "belief creates biology" is supported by this.

Thomas made the remark that the qualities and skills we display in life are trivial, like the tip of an iceberg, which started this conversation. I think it's now obvious to everyone why it was said that the majority were leaving the cemetery without having their interment music played.

Laughing, Jaleel remarked, "Nurturing mistakes and bad parenting." "According to behavioural specialists, up until puberty, parents and instructors subject children to pure conditioning for more than 25,000 hours. These, among other things, take the shape of stern words, gestures, looks, tones, and prohibitions that permanently leave the emotions and sensations that such programming created in their brains. The three main functions of the brain are recording, recall, and playback. At the right times in life, the conditionings and the accompanying sentiments would be recalled and replayed.

Sir, how does that happen?

When my mother asked if I could "do anything right, so my doing this is not going to be successful," the teacher would reply, "You are not even half-smart as your sister is, so there's no point in trying to do this task." I couldn't help being a bad guy since my father used to tell me, "You are a bad boy." These children's constant repetition of concepts aids in the formation of habits that would later have an impact on their way of life. As they become older, the "I'm not OK-you're OK" indoctrination tarnishes their personality. They will unintentionally write the story of their lives and live them out as a result. What will happen? a life that is largely lived alone since it hurts to be around people who are doing okay.

Supriya, what will happen to the neural network in such a situation? "Nurture won't win out against nature, sir. The synapses that connect the neurons will eventually get neglected, disregarded, and dissolve because they can be strengthened and aid individuals in developing talents.

Correct. Gifts entrusted to us by God at birth must be used in daily life to prevent being revoked by nature. Both nature and nurture have an impact on personality. Supriya said it well when she said "nurture will fail nature."

The self-confidence will erode as the "I'm not OK-You're OK" emotion becomes stronger, Remya said. One will consequently feel less deserving of themselves and be more prone to errors, rejection, and disappointment.

Sandeep, what will happen as a result of these cascades?Poor self-esteem makes it difficult to be motivated to learn new things or develop new abilities. He claimed that the personality strength would become ineffective if the gifts were not used and the mental connections deteriorated. That serves as both the justification and method by which people depart from this world empty-handed. Sandeep, that resolves the issue you brought up earlier. The instructor was done.

I feel as clear-headed about the world as a gooseberry in my hand right now. I used to wonder why some of the children who were born to Ashram devotees as a result of their "jivasuddhi" karma lacked particular skills and personality traits. It seems like the causes are now obvious, Malathi thought.

Malathi, there is still another important factor behind that. Anandavardhan gave his reply. disrespecting the great words of the Guru. As you are aware, Guru has emphasised time and time again that He will be powerless if His teachings are not faithfully obeyed. The consequences of disobeying the divine words in conformity with the global dharma would occur from nature, whether unintentionally or on design, and the Guru would not be able to stop them.

Parents and developing children frequently disregard this crucial guideline, which causes them to lose the life game. How do the Guru's remarks sound to you, sir? Supriya was seeking further information.

You can see that the Guru, who possesses supernatural insight into the past, present, and future, counsels you on how to lead a moral life. The Sanskrit word "Gu-ru" is literally translated as "remover of darkness." The Guru's guidelines for living are to be faithfully adhered to. Any departure from these will provoke the fury and wrath of nature.As we mentioned in the previous lesson, in order to properly profit from the spiritual practice of "jivasuddhi," malathi, first and foremost, punya (merit) in the jiva must be taken into account. Even the best intentions and efforts would fail if it is absent, according to Anandavardhan.

If you do your part, Sir, don't you suppose God will take care of the other half?According to Paramhamsa Yogananda, the first part of that proverb is also split in half.How do you feel about that?On the spiritual path, the devotee or disciple puts in 25% of the work, the guru puts in 25% of the effort, and the remaining 50% is the outcome of God's favour. It is even conceivable to say with absolute certainty that God, both in and through the Guru, accounts for 75% of the disciple's spiritual journey given that the Guru serves as a conduit to God. Those who follow the guru and consider him to be god will see that. You may also say that the jiva transmits the bhagya (God's grace), which makes up the other 50%.

Whether it be by the grace of the Supreme or the Guru's blessings, in either case, the disciple's twenty-five percent must be completed before requesting assistance from God. And you accomplish that by closely adhering to the Guru's instructions. Anandavardhan took a deep breath.

Please discuss a few more things concerning the life positions, sir. This is the question: "What are they?"The top spot is obvious. What factors, though, will cause a young youngster to advance to position two or three?

Around the ninth month of pregnancy, what happens?Let's investigate. A child changes from being a baby to a toddler when they turn one. Up to the age of one, a person is still regarded as a baby, which is a stage that is extraordinarily rich in admiration and love. The baby stage ends when the infant learns to stand and walk in the tenth month, and the toddler stage begins. Between the ages of one and two, it will continue. Toddlers might be identified by their awkward, unsteady steps.

Although the child enjoys the process of learning to walk, he also begins to experience some undesirable side effects at that time. Up until that time, his parents and others had cradled and cuddled him for the duration of his life. He is immediately "grounded," and the parents' hugging and cuddling are diminished or stopped. Additionally, when he starts to use his recently discovered locomotive freedom, he encounters "strange" and unfriendly parents.

As he enjoys his tremendous freedom, the child starts snatching and breaking countless objects right there and then. And the parents respond with their first-ever reprimands and scowling looks. Why did you touch it? Why do you take things and destroy them when they are not required? Why can't you sit down and play with the toys that were given to you? can occasionally also be punished with minor offences.

What follows is what? The toddler's perspective of others changes as a result of these novel experiences and the emotions they elicit. You are not okay. As he moves forward, he encounters unpleasant comments and consequences as well as bodily injuries and bruises from falling down, and he cries out, "I'm not OK-you're not OK." The toddler firmly anchors in this new life position and cognitively crafts a new life script when these events happen frequently enough.

Parents are the centre of the universe for newborns and early children. But instead of all-stroking, all-loving, and all-attentive, the world is now all-off-bosom, negative-stroking, berating, blaming, and beating to a toddler. Even if he occasionally experiences praise and affection from his parents or other people in the gaps between the brand-new, horrific episodes, he won't be content with such fleeting experiences. He will hold onto this fresh feeling and declare, "I'm not OK; you're not OK."

# Criminals Do Not Appear Out Of Nowhere

Let's now assess the evolution of the third life position. If a child is treated unfairly, harshly, intentionally, or brutally by their parents or other adults, it is understandable that they will feel rejected. Additionally, he decides "I'm OK" because he must remain silent while enduring the cruelties of these "six-feat fall" strong people.

It is general knowledge that having a nasty stepmother or stepfather has a negative impact on the majority of children. These days, it's not uncommon to hear tales of a selfish mother wanting to run away from her children so she may hide and pursue an illicit relationship or even a biological father abusing a teenage daughter. These youths also exhibit the "I'm OK—you're not OK" mentality.A Malayalam film's protagonist is a character like the one you described, sir. Because of his teenage experiences, he adopted this way of life.

Jaleel, why do you continually bring up fictitious characters? The most well-known historical illustration of this paradigm shift in human existence is Adolf Hitler. If Hitler had a nice upbringing and youth, history as we know it today would be very different.You brought up, sir, how the child implied, "I'm OK." Self-stroking must be the cause of such a favourable self-perception. How on earth can a two or three year old praise themselves? Sandeep enquired.

Outstanding question. If and when children who are treated in an extremely cruel, brutal, and continuously degrading manner by their guardians or the like manage to overcome such ordeals by stoicism and survival instinct, they will find peace and solace in being by themselves. They will be relieved that they survived the hardest time in their lives. They believe that if you just leave them alone, everything will be fine. You're not fine since you caused me physical and mental harm.

The survivor who is prepared for the worst won't give up. The phrase "I'm OK-You're not OK" can practically save a child's life. But what will happen to this egregiously neglected child when he grows up? He'll respond by striking. not just at his assailants, but also at society at large. This crime was committed and is still being committed by Hitler and other terrible criminals.

This is how bad parenting affects the following generation. The damaged child won't look inside as he gets older. Instead, he'll ruminate on his past on a regular basis, saying things like, "It's them," "They're the bad guys," or "They're the wreckers." With this vengeful mindset, he will consider himself as always OK and everyone else as always wrong, not just toward his wrongdoers but also toward society as a whole. Since treating such a moral moron would make the doctor appear to be one of "the others" and would be unacceptable, no corrective action is possible. He finally changes into a criminal as a result. What also sparked the beginning of this tragedy? astonishing lack of food! the abuse of children

# Most Ideal Environment For An Existence

Also, sir, could you please explain the fourth position. The ideal relationship is "I'm OK-You're OK." A mature individual who respects themselves and others is one indication of maturity. This position is fundamentally different from the other three. As we've seen, the first three are imprinted emotions that develop and persist throughout childhood. We also learnt that almost everyone is accidentally trapped in one of these jobs for the rest of their lives. These feelings have only been based on these emotions or experiences; no additional information has been used to confirm or authenticate them.

The fourth position, I'm OK-You're OK, on the other hand, is founded on thought, faith, and confidence in deed. We don't just express ourselves verbally based on our sentiments; we also pick what to say. Being intellectually mature, the individual in this position thinks "why not?", as opposed to the preceding three, which just answer the question "why?" (helpless recipient and beholder). He selects after some thought.

Why, sir, was it impossible to change an unconscious thought that had formed and become established in early childhood despite acquiring knowledge and life experience?

It's a well-known axiom of Aristotelian philosophy that "what is said will get imprinted. One's heart will never experience a feeling that hasn't been experienced in its purest form before the age of three. The only possible exception might be something sexual or similar.

We discovered that the brain's main job is to constantly record events. In addition to the actual event, the brain's high-fidelity tape recorder will also capture the emotions associated with the encounter. Additionally, it would replicate the special emotion by reliving the encounter in real time. Your brain won't forget an experience, even if your conscious mind does. The incident and the associated feeling would both be vividly remembered at the same time.

Does the brain store every moment since conception for future review? Or is a specific age range its exclusive target audience?Suhra, it's not simply at birth. Beginning in the seventh month of pregnancy, the brain would register each interaction. It is suggestive of this scientific truth when Mahabharatha claims that Abhimanyu was able to remember the specifics of entering the Chakravyuh at the right time in the battlefield when he was sixteen years old by remembering what he heard and his brain registered during the prenatal stage.

"Wow! Maharshi Veda Vyasa deserves praise for his extensive scientific expertise on this topic.Supriya claimed to be shocked. "The discoveries on the cosmos and the origin of life made by modern scientists, working with the opulent accompaniment of a multitude of ultramodern pieces of equipment and techniques, will pale into utter insignificance when compared to the wisdom and insight our ancient seers used to reveal, thousands of years ago, the workings of the universe and the secrets behind every form of life on this planet. Supriya, in addition to our genuflecting, Vyas Maharshi requires our complete submission and prostrations.

As you put it, sir.On top of that, we are told that in the past, Charaka or Sushrutha could diagnose illnesses just by feeling or touching the body's essential organs, hearing the heartbeat (Of course without a stethoscope), and performing other similar tasks. They lacked ECG, CT, X-ray, and comparable apparatus. The founder of modern medicine, Hippocrates, frequently recognized in his writings that he had learned pharmacology, materia medica, etc. from these prehistoric doctors. That is the ingenuity of the ancient Indians' insight and wisdom.

# Analysis Of A Case

Now, take attention to a few case studies that Dr. Thomas Harris has provided, which attest to the fact that until a conscious decision is made to change it, a person's life will be lived in accordance with the life position they constructed as children.

Once, a woman of forty crossed the street recklessly. She was unexpectedly interrupted by a certain genre of menacing music emanating from a local music store. The depressing song hit her right away, leaving her feeling disheartened. Her eyes began to tear up. Despite her dismay, she persisted, but she abandoned the rest of her plans and went home. But as the days passed, her melancholy deepened and she completely lost herself in the music.

She went to the doctor for assistance when she began to feel drowsy. He questioned her about any childhood memories that involved such depressing music. She was out of them, the woman objected. But at the conclusion of the week, she told him that the song had unintentionally brought back a memory from when she was a very little girl.

Her mother used to perform this song in front of the piano when she was a small girl, doing so in a charming and passionate manner. She was five years old when her mother passed away, and it came as a huge blow to her. Despite her family's best attempts, she was so miserable that no one could ever fill the vacuum in her life.

I used to keep humming the song to myself for a very long time after that since I used to remember my mum singing it as she was seated in front of the piano. Then, as time passed, this recollection vanished entirely. A week ago, I heard it again in front of that music store. As time passed, she started to remember 2005, when she had expressed her want for her mother to the doctor.

The doctor asked, "Do you now feel okay?" "Yeah. I feel better and have changed since I now know why I was experiencing those unpleasant feelings," she stated.

It is clear from this instance that the woman's recollection of a 35-year-old incident was reignited by the young girl's strong emotions. This episode shows how the brain records, recalls, and replays experiences.

Let's now consider the viewpoint of a teen's mother. She followed a particular household rule that her mother had taught her when she was a young girl with zeal. She made it a rule that visitors couldn't leave their jackets or hats on the bed or the table. She would criticise everyone who unintentionally broke the rule, driving her crazy in the process.

The youngster carefully carried out her mother's directions as well. The woman once questioned her elderly mother as to why she had been brought up with this seemingly illogical rule. That was because my mother had warned me as a child not to put their hats on our table or their jackets on our beds after numerous of the neighbourhood kids caught a contagious fever. Remya remarked, "Habits die hard, and I taught it to you as well to protect us from infections.

Additionally, Anandavardhan noted, the kids were teaching them beliefs. We adhere to many different paradigms throughout life. Since we were taught these concepts, we never challenge their accuracy. And we always do as instructed by our parents.

Why, sir, are encounters of this nature never put to the test before being adopted as a norm, a guideline, or a law? Malathi, how is that possible? How can a two-foot-tall, uneducated, and illiterate youngster challenge the knowledge of a six-foot-tall, all-knowing, and well-versed parent? The child believes that the parent is constantly in good health, yet they are never in good health. Let's assume he asks, "Why?" while continuing to bob his head. What will remain the primary theme? Simply adhere to the directions. It should not be placed on the table, that is all the hat's message. Avoid asking "why."

Many people nodded their heads in agreement. Let's talk about what it's like for a modern housewife who has access to all but a waste disposal unit of the mechanical kitchen equipment. not because she was unable to pay for it. In fact, she frequently overheard her husband suggesting that they buy one. The woman didn't appear to care, though. Her husband gave her a thorough description of how a garbage disposal machine might organise the kitchen, streamline tasks, and save time. Every argument he had was known to his wife, but she didn't care.

The partner was in need. One day, he asked her why she didn't want to have a waste disposal installed in the house. The wife began to question her stern stance for the first time. She questioned herself, wondering what was wrong with this convenience. Why should it be despised? She spent numerous days searching the shadows for an explanation. After the tracking mission was over, she thought back to an incident from her adolescence.

She was born in the 1930s, at the height of the Great Depression. Her parents, who came from a lower middle class family, made it a point to meticulously save garbage so they could feed the pigs when they were killed around Christmas. It gave the family food and a large amount of income. So that the dishwater, along with the slope and other nutritious leftovers, could be thrown out, even the kitchen's dishes were washed without soap.

She used to believe that trash had value and shouldn't be thrown away when she was a little child. She had been brought up with this deeply ingrained belief, therefore it was challenging for her to comprehend the concept of disposing of kitchen waste using a garbage disposal device. She always had to say "no" whenever her husband brought up the notion due to the childhood memories and ideas it evoked about the value of kitchen waste. Did hearing this increase her sense of reason and comprehension when it was explained to her?

Yes. She altered her attitude and happily decided to purchase and begin using a garbage disposal. The second woman also altered her perception of where the hat or coat should be placed on the bed and table.

# A Man Is Made By His Mind

Let's look at what these paradigm shifts involve. The professor switched on the projector and opened a paper on his laptop. On the screen behind him, the iceberg was once more discernible. He made two or three full circles around the iceberg while holding the laser pointer in his palm.

"Up to this point, we've talked about the reasons why human skill and potential are underutilised by 90%. And we discovered that early childhood indoctrination is the main culprit behind the same.

However, there are many parallels between individuals and the iceberg. More is involved than that. Any further hunches?

The class was once more enveloped in icy silence. The iceberg on the screen was the focus of thirty pairs of eyes.

"Malathi, do you remember the Guruvani in which Guru highlighted three things on which purity has to be developed?" demanded Anandavardhan.

Heart, mouth, and actions, please. You will begin to love God if they become more pure, and God will begin to love you.

The Guruvani and the mantra "mind, words, and deeds" were uttered by Anandavardhan. His cursor circled the iceberg once more. Suhra lifted her hand from the rear of the room. "The iceberg represents the human mind, words, and deeds," she stated as she stood up. Like the unseen majority of the iceberg, the mind is a portion of ourselves that is invisible to others. The words and behaviours are only the tip of the iceberg in terms of what the world may see and hear.

"Correct response. Why did the Guru encourage us to pursue cleanliness of mind, heart, and body? The teacher questioned Malathi. She responded, "So that the person will be absolutely spotless." The instructor counselled, "Once you achieve purity in thought, word, and deed, you will be so near God that your true love will flow towards the Almighty and so too will God's love to you.

A person's mentality must be thoroughly cleansed before anything else. One must be aware of everything in their mind that has to be cleansed in order to achieve this. The mind is where thoughts, emotions, and inferences all begin. It serves as a repository for ideas, emotions, and impressions. They make up the mentality collectively. Through one's face, words, attitudes, and actions, these interior factors will be expressed to others. the virtue that arises from internal holiness.

Because of this, it is believed that each word and each concept is a seed from which a deed will grow. Whether a fruit will be good or terrible is determined by its seed. The bulk of a person's attitude can create or break his personality, much as how the majority of an iceberg is invisible to the unaided sight. Certainly not, Sir?

That's all. There is no denying the size of the human mind given how much it affects the entire body. The actions, statements, and demonstrations are merely the "tip of the iceberg." A person's thought is responsible for 80% of their achievements.

"True," I replied. "Attitude determines altitude." Parents contribute 80% of a child's attitudinal intelligence. The rest of the kids learn via their professors, their surroundings, their culture, etc. In other words, a person's traits are influenced by both nature and nurture. The parents' wisdom and discernment are essential.

According to a specialist in this field, mental intelligence is initially developed in adolescents up to the age of 18 before they use it. His personality will have largely stabilised by then. It will require significant mental alterations to be further altered or improved.

Up until the third year of life, a child's viewpoints are formed based on their experiences, and as a result, their life position is firmly defined. Because perceptions are the starting point for attitudes, perceptions serve as the "raw materials" from which attitudes are "manufactured." The calibre of the raw materials used in the manufacture of any product determines its standard. As soon as the perspective shifts, so will the attitude, along with the words and deeds.

We discovered that in the case scenarios, the women's attitudes and behaviours changed along with those of the cap, coat, and waste disposal equipment.

A person's actions and words always support how they are seen. What word would you use, Remya, to define this quality in people?The phrase "self-fulfilling prophecy"Yeah.Malathi stated, "Due to this, Guru instructed the disciples at the ashram to never consider or say that the Kaliyuga was a terrible age. It is described as "a person's unconscious attempt to demonstrate the truth of his internal dialogues, which emerge from his perception, through his behaviours and actions."

# Education And Inspiration

"Isn't the prevalent perception of Kaliyuga only negative? People frequently point the finger at the present Kaliyuga when things go wrong or crimes are committed. The contradicting claims made by Malathi shocked Supriya.

Anandavardhan remarked, "The spiritual master takes exception to that." Several of the guru's indoctrinations require the followers and devotees to thoroughly unlearn. Unlearning is what, sir?

We previously discovered there are two ways to learn: through personal experience and through absorbing knowledge from others. There are three main methods of education. One is acquiring knowledge or learning new things via the two approaches listed above. The second method entails removing from memory some knowledge that you had previously ingested but now feel is incorrect or invalid. This procedure is referred to as "unlearning."

Tell me more, sir. OK. Let's take one as an illustration. Consider purchasing an aquarium. a vast body of water with a giant fish. A glass divider is then placed in the middle of the tank and split in half. Currently, the fish are using half of the aquarium. There are currently a lot of minnows in the other region. These tiny fish are swimming around the aquarium with joy.

The big fish on the other side will extend its jaws to grab the minnows as they swim by and get close to the glass wall. The fish retreats after making its first contact with the wall and failing to capture its prey. All that actually happened was that they kept trying and going back. After a few days of this fruitless attempt, the gigantic fish would finally give up its false optimism and quit the activities. The big fish will just ignore the minnows as they swim near to the wall and go about their business.

You now carefully remove the glass panel that had been separating the two sections of the aquarium. With a bigger swimming area, the huge fish and the minnows can both travel around without restriction. The minnows swim right up to the 'enemy's' mouth and slide through, blissfully oblivious to the impending threat of being sucked. The enormous fish never opens its mouth to take a meal. Experience is the reason. The fish now believes that it is impossible to capture any minnows.Yeah. The large fish's brain strongly believes that the minnows cannot be caught at all after numerous days of futile attempts to do so. It has given up on the concept as a result. Can the fish possibly eat the smaller ones?

It must alter how it sees the circumstances. It must give up the concept it has stored in its head. It should be aware of how simple it is to catch minnows today. Remya responded.

How, though? The preceding learning must be lost if anything needs to be learned that clashes with what is already stored in the brain. That implies that the prior information must be forgotten. Unlearning is the deliberate attempt to forget what has already been learned.

The catch is that the fish cannot consciously decide to unlearn. Humans are the only members of the animal kingdom with self-awareness and conscience, while fish do not possess these traits.

What does unlearning entail in terms of education, in your opinion?First, realise the distinction between forgetting and unlearning. It is not an intentional choice to forget. Anything that you are aware of, you won't forget. The purposeful process of trying to forget or delete previously learned information from memory is known as unlearning. As a result, you are consciously learning to unlearn. Due to the fact that it follows established learning procedures, it naturally qualifies as a teaching strategy.

Successful unlearning leaves a knowledge gap that can be filled with fresh material. Re-learning, the third technique of learning, is the process of learning something new in place of something that hasn't been learned.

Is it correct to suggest that the women in the case stories relearned their initial impressions of the hat, coat, and garbage disposal device after unlearning them?Correct. Willfully forgetting what you've already learnt is difficult. Forgetting something is often difficult as well, especially if it is something you value deeply or is a quality or behaviour you inherited from your ancestors. Such deeply ingrained knowledge and ideas will require a person to have enormous resolve, willpower, and the capacity to overcome resistance from family members who disagree with the concept of giving it up as well as from their own self-consciousness.

In response, Malathi said, "Sir, most of the time, it will be easier for people who have little formal education to do such unlearning than their learned and scholarly counterparts." The Ashram adequately demonstrates that. "How?" Remya expressed interest.

"Our Guru wished to reform the worship of multiple deities as well as the improper rites and customs that were used in the devotion, which belonged in past ages. Malathi argued that whereas educated and higher class individuals resisted understanding the truth and substance of the Master's teachings, the illiterate and semi-literate disciples had no such reluctance or reservations about internalising and taking the Guru's instructions seriously.

# Education Weakens Inherent Intelligence

"Even scientific studies have demonstrated that your natural intelligence will decline as you progress in book learning." Sir, give a detailed definition of natural intelligence. "Have you ever observed how skillfully birds construct their nests? Which even the top architects and engineers would be envious of?

Have you ever wondered why geese fly in an inverted V pattern across the sky, which enables them to go more quickly while using less energy? What about beavers, squirrels, and ants—all those intelligent animals? These are all examples of the intelligence that is innate in animals and birds. Where do individuals go to learn about or receive instruction in this useful skill of sensible living? The greatest management institutes in the world would be in awe of their astounding exhibition of innate genius and capacity to understand even the most difficult or esoteric nuances of practical knowledge.

They have a very high innate intelligence—what's the secret, sir? Why don't we have anything comparable, then?Simple. The birds and animals don't have the same formal education and training that we do. Early-onset conditioning and straight-jacketing have the effect of eradicating people's innate intelligence and inventiveness.

How would you explain the fact that this has been recognised by the scientific community?The scenario is as follows: A child begins in kindergarten. Studies claim that by the time he finishes 20 years of formal education and earns a Ph.D. or equivalent, about 70% of his native IQ will have been irretrievably lost.

Guru claims that as a result, those with the highest levels of education display the most idiocy. Malathi piped in again, "There will be no chaff in the Master's teachings."

This is accurate since egos grow as a result of learning. Due to the ego's interaction with the mind, we will then be unable to know the truth. Any knowledge that opposes and goes beyond his schooling won't be able to be absorbed and comprehended by someone with such a focus on books.

According to Anandavardhan, those who have an open mind are the only ones who can be sensitive and creative since their way of thinking is, "the more I know, the more I know I don't know."

You change your thinking into "Sir, kindly revert to self-fulfilling prophecy, which needs some more explaining" as a result of it.OK. Malathi invoked the Guru when she urged us not to believe the falsehood that the Kaliyuga is evil. This is due to the fact that having a strong opinion about something may unintentionally affect the way that you speak, behave, and act.

The brain cannot tell the difference between reality and fiction. Whether or not they are true, it just adopts our opinions without examination and creates a cosmos that supports them. "Yadh bhavam, thadh bhavathi" is a Sanskrit proverb that translates to "things will turn out as you perceive them within." Ipso facto, you can only guess what will happen if you think the Age you're in is terrible. You'll demonstrate the validity of your assertion with your life. Self-fulfilling prophecy is the act of your internal predictions or prophecies coming true.

Every time something goes wrong in the community, whether it be injustice, crime, riot, or other inflicted pain, people have developed the practice of retiring to the simulated area of safety and stating that this is Kali. All of the crimes and atrocities performed by influential parties will be seen as the natural result of the wrong Age that we are destined to live in. Nothing practical can be done to stop or prevent such grave threats to the ability of society to live in peace. The aforementioned teaching of the Guru becomes extremely important in this context.

Don't you agree, Sir, that a person's attitude determines their life and future? It either acts as the primary force for all development and expansion or acts in direct opposition to it. The boys' lives were spared by Dharmaputra's actions during the incident in the bush.Yeah. Because of this, Guru always cautioned us to be careful about our daily mental states. He also suggested that we routinely evaluate our attitudes by using a useful strategy.

# Journaling For Self-Reflection

"What's the tool?" you ask. People have recently been encouraged to do so by psychologists and life management specialists from all around the world. which the Guru had previously suggested. Malathi, do you still remember it?

Don't just think about the past. I do that as well. Malathi exclaimed as she stood up. She ascended and greeted the pupils with enthusiasm. "Make a list of all the significant events and happenings from the day each evening before you go to bed. Your thoughts and feelings, your interactions with others and what happened to you while you were with them, all of the significant things you did, your emotional states throughout the day, etc.

Rather than merely stating the facts as they are, it does more. You must also think about your actions and evaluate all of the data that was recorded. By doing this, you can create a personal mirror picture of your thoughts. It's akin to how blind your own eyes are to yourself. You can only see your thinking in such faithful words, just like you can only see your eyes in a mirror.

You may then alter your thoughts, feelings, words, and behaviours by doing this. Your interpersonal and professional connections will improve as a result. The personality will thereby substantially advantage. Then, isn't that journal writing ?Supriya enquired.

The trainer emphasised journaling, not keeping a notebook. What exactly distinguishes the two? "A journal is nothing more than an accurate account of the events of the day. It turns into a journal when you add your own value to it through critical analysis, evaluation, judgement, and inference. In addition to your personal observations and inferences drawn as a result of inquiries like "what," "why," and "how," it will search for solutions to these questions and their variations. In other words, the notebook will contain a person's daily self-evaluation. Keeping a journal will promote mental growth and in-depth thought if you do it with sincerity, honesty, and objectivity. Scientific research has also backed up its advantages. It is asked, "What are they?"

A person's immune system, health, and attitude can all be improved by simply writing in a notebook for fifteen minutes each day, according to studies. More unforeseen advantages exist.

The speaker explained, "You must first comprehend the anatomy of writing in order to understand it. The pupils were attentive and occupied with taking notes. When you write something, your muscles, hand nerves, and intellect are all being used. It involves the psycho-neuro-muscular system. Because writing concurrently involves all three of these areas of your body, whatever you write down on paper will also be immediately remembered in your memory.

Do you recall the Aristotelian idea we discussed earlier? It declares that words have the power to leave an impression. It also holds true in the other sense: what is said will also impress. Here, one can express their ideas and diary entries through regular activities.

That implies that attitudes and behaviours will change, right?Yeah. Everyone should keep a daily journal, the Guru advised, and they should "put certain things about daily life into black and white and keep it." Your morning's initial emotional state, the results—both good and bad—the number and kind of interactions you had, your overall behaviours, etc. Participation in this is encouraged for everyone who wishes to devote their entire lives to the Ashram.

You may yet see superb management in this great spiritual master despite the fact that he had minimal formal education. As I indicated before, management professionals are today repeating what the Guru said decades ago.

For example, the eminent corporate trainer, consultant, and globetrotter Robin Sharma is credited with the proverbial line: "If your life is worth thinking about, it is worth writing about." Along with a large number of other authors from throughout the world, he highlights the significance of journaling as a self-development tool.

I believe it promotes self-evaluation, Sir. Remya stepped in.Exactly. It can be developed as a process and instrument for practical personal development.

We may get the conclusion that the mind is the most important component. A person's outward appearance is influenced by how they feel on the inside. It's possible to succeed in life from the inside out.

Consider showing some love to your inner life mate, who joined you while your mother was carrying you and will undoubtedly stick by your side until the very end. It helps to mould who you are and offers the possibility to make a lasting impression. I refer to one's inner "self." Sadly, we usually feed our egos rather than our true selves. Even while both are a part of our subtle body, the ego tends to "edge" the good out. Because all of your earliest creations are formed in the mind, it has a tendency to identify more with the self.

When engaging with others, people typically adopt one of four life stances: "I'm not OK-You're OK," "I'm OK-You're OK," "I'm OK-You're not OK," and "I'm OK-You're OK." When a child's parents, who are their universe's centre, meet their needs, they regard him as lacking and not OK while the others see him as OK.

When the child enters the tenth month of life, begins to walk independently, and begins to play tricks, the quantity of love and attention from the parents decreases. Additionally, he receives his first sarcastic looks, punches, and other sorts of berating. As a result, he develops a second-life viewpoint and begins to regard his parents and other people as sharing many of the same defects as himself.

The child alters his perspective to believe that "I'm OK-You're not OK" in the all-too-rare circumstance where he is subject to abuse, brutality, and horrors and finds himself helpless, unable to revolt, and left to mend for himself.

One of these three points of view will have firmly taken root as an unspoken, non-verbal conclusion about life by the time a child reaches the age of three. After that, it can only be altered through deliberate choice. Every human being possesses all three states of being. Based on one's life experiences, one develops into a child, parent, and adult. These memories, along with the emotions they sparked, are perfectly preserved in the brain, from which they may be accurately retrieved and replayed.

The Child state and Parent state begin in infancy, whereas the Adult state begins around the ninth month of life. The taught concept of life serves as the foundation for the Parent state, the thought concept of life serves as the foundation for the Adult state, and the felt concept of life that is stored in the brain serves as the foundation for the Child state.

Unlike the conceived idea, which is documented from the ninth month on, the felt concept and the taught concept are documented from birth to age five. These three ideas have a significant lifetime effect and permanently alter the neural pathways in the brain. In all four life roles, there are interactions between the child, parent, and adult perceptions of persons.

The personalities of the children will suffer if their parents and teachers impose too many limitations, restrictions, and conditionings. Children and teenagers need encouragement, motivation, and positive reinforcement just as much as they need nutritious food.

The young youngster consciously chooses the fourth life position, I'm OK-You're OK. A youngster that develops with this mentality will become an independent, assertive, and deserving adult. Biology is influenced by belief. The outside expressions of internal beliefs, perceptions, and conclusions gained from experiences include words, acts, and deeds. The former will make the changes required by the latter.

We frequently engage in the three learning stages of learning, unlearning, and relearning in order to increase our knowledge. An unconscious attempt to use one's words and actions to reinforce one's own thoughts and beliefs is known as a self-fulfilling prophecy. It is frequently false and in conflict with reality.

It is crucial to regularly assess our mental health so that any necessary adjustments can be made right away. Journaling can help people create a culture where they regularly evaluate their personalities and selves.

The importance of constantly monitoring one's thinking has been emphasised by the spiritual teacher as a way to raise one's standard of living and relationships with others. He suggested keeping a journal as a tool for this. The mind is most important since one's mental state shapes who they are.

# Don't miss out!

Visit the website below and you can sign up to receive emails whenever Book Wave Publications publishes a new book. There's no charge and no obligation.

https://books2read.com/r/B-A-LAFAB-MXUNC

BOOKS 2 READ

Connecting independent readers to independent writers.

# Also by Book Wave Publications

How To Make Money In Stocks Value Investing Strategies
Master The Steps To Move Away From The Past And
Following Inspiration
Heartful Journeys: Exploring The Power Of Mindful Living